G is for Genes

Understanding Children's Worlds
Series Editor: Judy Dunn

The study of children's development can have a profound influence on how children are brought up, cared for and educated. Many psychologists argue that, even if our knowledge is incomplete, we have a responsibility to attempt to help those concerned with the care, education and study of children by making what we know available to them. The central aim of this series is to encourage developmental psychologists to set out the findings and the implications of their research for others – teachers, doctors, social workers, students and fellow researchers – whose work involves the care, education and study of young children and their families. The information and the ideas that have grown from recent research form an important resource which should be available to them. This series provides an opportunity for psychologists to present their work in a way that is interesting, intelligible and substantial, and to discuss what its consequences may be for those who care for, and teach children: not to offer simple prescriptive advice to other professionals, but to make important and innovative research accessible to them.

G is for Genes

The Impact of Genetics on Education and Achievement

Kathryn Asbury and Robert Plomin

WILEY Blackwell

This edition first published 2014
© 2014 John Wiley & Sons, Inc.

Registered Office
John Wiley & Sons Ltd, The Atrium, Southern Gate, Chichester,
West Sussex, PO19 8SQ, UK

Editorial Offices
350 Main Street, Malden, MA 02148-5020, USA
9600 Garsington Road, Oxford, OX4 2DQ, UK
The Atrium, Southern Gate, Chichester, West Sussex, PO19 8SQ, UK

For details of our global editorial offices, for customer services,
and for information about how to apply for permission to reuse the
copyright material in this book please see our website at
www.wiley.com/wiley-blackwell.

Library of Congress Cataloging-in-Publication Data

Asbury, Kathryn.
G is for genes : the impact of genetics on education and achievement / Kathryn Asbury
and Robert Plomin.
pages cm. – (Understanding children's worlds ; 13)
Includes bibliographical references and index.
ISBN 978-1-118-48278-0 (hardback) – ISBN 978-1-118-48281-0 (paperback)
1. Learning ability–Genetic aspects. 2. Academic achievement. 3. Behavior genetics.
I. Plomin, Robert, 1948– II. Title.
LB1134.A83 2013
370.15′23–dc23
2013017491

A catalogue record for this book is available from the British Library.

Cover image: © nathan Knowles / Getty Images
Cover design by www.cyandesign.co.uk

Typeset in 10.5/14pt Sabon by Laserwords Private Limited, Chennai, India
Printed in Malaysia by Ho Printing (M) Sdn Bhd

1 2014

For the TEDS families, with thanks

The Universe is not going to see someone like you again in the entire history of creation.

Vartan Gregorian

Contents

x   Contents

Acknowledgements

This book began as an idea several years ago, and its writing has been informed and inspired by discussions with generous colleagues at London's Institute of Psychiatry ever since, for which we thank them. Our field, behavioral genetics, is developing at considerable speed and we look forward to continuing and extending those discussions in tandem with new developments in both genetics and education.

The writing of *G is for Genes* was made possible by funding from the British Academy in the form of a Postdoctoral Fellowship awarded to KA, and our research into the school environment is funded by the US National Institutes of Health. We thank both bodies for believing in the importance of this endeavor.

We thank Peter Tallack of The Science Factory, and Professor Judy Dunn for their invaluable support and encouragement as we prepared to submit our draft manuscript for publication. Both contributed ideas which have made *G is for Genes* a better book, and both were a pleasure to work with. Thanks also to Nick Asbury for coming up with our title.

A particularly special thank you is owed to Jonah Asbury who helped in ways too numerous to mention but, in particular, we thank him for his generously given editorial advice which was always "on the money." Finally, we thank the thousands of families who make up the Twins' Early Development Study (TEDS). We have dedicated our book to these families because, although we have become accustomed to their generosity, it really is astonishing that they find time in their busy lives to contribute to science and society on such a regular basis. They make our research possible and we are eternally grateful.

Part One
In Theory

Chapter 1

Genetics, Schools, and Learning

The science of genetics is changing our world at an ever-increasing pace. We can now analyze and modify DNA to test for serious illnesses and treat them before they become life-threatening, to catch criminals and exonerate the innocent, and to create energy sources that will protect our planet. Geneticists have cast their nets far and wide to influence and inform medicine and public health, agriculture, energy and the environment, law, and social policy. Education, however, is glaringly absent from this list, and schools remain untouched by the lessons of genetics. This, we believe, needs to change.

One way of helping each and every child to fulfill their academic potential is to harness the lessons of genetic research. We now know a great deal – though not by any means everything – about the ways that genes influence learning, and about how children's DNA interacts with their experiences at home and school. It's time for educationalists and policy makers to sit down with geneticists to apply these findings to educational practice. It will make for better

G is for Genes: The Impact of Genetics on Education and Achievement, First Edition.
Kathryn Asbury and Robert Plomin.
© 2014 John Wiley & Sons, Inc. Published 2014 by John Wiley & Sons, Inc.

schools, thriving children, and, in the long run, a more fulfilled and effective population. That's what we want schools and education to achieve, isn't it?

The Aims and Assumptions of Education

Like most areas of public policy, education is a hotbed of disagreements and competing philosophies. Fundamentally, however, we can all agree that education should give everybody the basic tools they need to function in society. In most of the world right now these tools, or skills, consist of reading, writing, arithmetic, and an ability to interact with digital technologies. We can probably identify a secondary aim: only the most extreme libertarian would object to the notion that societies should benefit in tangible ways from providing education to their citizens. A recent OECD report for instance claimed that if all OECD countries could equal the average educational performance of the Finns the combined financial gain over the course of a single generation, the generation born in 2010, would be $115 trillion. By 2090 the gain would increase to $260 trillion. Both the United States and the United Kingdom would be among the nations to gain most in these economic terms, along with Mexico, Turkey, Italy, Germany, Spain and France. It is noteworthy that the Finnish education system puts a particularly high premium on basic skills and has a comparatively small gap between its most and least able pupils. Of course, education should not restrict itself to these two aims: the first is the bare minimum to which a society, a school, or a teacher should aspire, and the second is a by-product of the first. If these aims are not achieved then we may have icing but we have no cake.

The simple aims of learning to read, write, calculate, and use a computer are achievable by virtually every member of society regardless of their IQ. If even one child (not including those with profound disabilities but including those with, for instance, mild and moderate learning, emotional, or behavioral difficulties) leaves school without achieving an acceptable level of competence in these skills, then their school and the education system supporting it have failed them. This is entirely unacceptable.

Sadly these aims are not always met: young people sometimes do leave school insufficiently literate and numerate even after 11 years (15,000 hours) of full-time education. The prospect of these young people becoming happy, fulfilled, and useful members of society is bleak. When this happens everybody blames everybody else, with excuses running from fractured societies through inner city schools with jaded teachers, unsupportive parents, low ability, and poor behavior . . . impossible kids in impossible circumstances basically. This is a cop-out. There is something far more fundamental going on. The entire education system is predicated on the belief that children are "blank slates." Behavioral genetics tells us that this is wrong.

This theory of education (and of human life in general) says that children are all born the same, with exactly the same potential, and become the product of their experiences. They are blank slates to be written upon by families, schools, and society. Many people believe that if their children behave well it is because they bring them up well; that if they are successful in school it is because they have excellent teachers and supportive parents. Conversely, they believe that if children play truant or display antisocial behavior their parents and teachers are at fault and should be held responsible, to the extent, in the case of parents, of being sentenced to terms of imprisonment. At a less extreme level this belief causes people doing a perfectly decent job of bringing up their children to torture themselves. Is he anxious because I mollycoddle him? Is she bossy because I give her too much attention? Is she two reading levels behind the neighbor's son because I didn't get her into the popular and over-subscribed school down the road? Should I have arranged a tutor to prepare him for selective school entrance exams? This kind of environmental determinism has become the norm, with all of the smugness and censure that it inevitably entails.

However, if you ask any parent of more than one child whether their babies were blank slates at birth or whether each child arrived with their own bundle of obvious traits – namely their temperament, appetites, needs, and preferences – you will hear the same reply. They were individuals from the moment they were born. If we took all babies from their families at birth and raised them in identical, government-sponsored rearing camps they would not resemble each other much more than they do now on school entry, and the resemblance would fade further as they grew and developed. People sometimes assume that environmental influence becomes more important as we develop and accumulate experiences. However, for traits such as cognitive development the reverse appears to be true. Genetic influence increases over time until, in later life, cognitive ability is almost as heritable as height.

The fact that individual differences are influenced by genes makes a lie of the blank slate philosophy. This in turn means that "more of the same" is unlikely to be the correct approach for children who are failing to stock up their toolkit of basic skills through ordinary means. A child who is not learning in the usual way can almost always be helped to learn, but their teachers may have to think outside the box and use their knowledge and experience of teaching and of the individual child to find the right buttons to push. They also need to be supported by policies that allow them to work this way.

To provide all children with a basic toolkit for life it is undoubtedly true that one vital focus of any education system has to be on making sure no child is left behind. Such a simple, clear aim has simple, clear policy implications: target resources at the children who struggle to equip themselves with basic academic tools and help them by whatever means work for them as individuals. The first funding priority for education should be to provide whatever is required to give every child enough facility with words, numbers, and computers to be able to live an independent life in the twenty-first century. Extra funding must be provided to help those children who struggle to meet these standards before they leave school, whatever the reason for their failure to progress. This may be one way in which we can start to tackle the challenge of improving social mobility in nations such as the United States and the United Kingdom. An emphasis on supporting those who need support to learn the basics is just a starting point, however.

In societies where education is freely available and compulsory for all children, pupils can be differentiated by the way in which they respond to instruction. The ability to learn from teachers is, we know, influenced more by genes than by experience. The influence of school on differences between children in how well they achieve is likely to be larger in societies where the availability of formal education is unequal. It is understandable, then, that in developed nations we find higher estimates of genetic influence, and lower estimates of the impact of schooling, on individual differences in achievement. If access to education is the same for everybody it cannot explain the differences between individuals. Formal education, standardized to be the same in all classrooms, can form the bedrock on which the bell curve of ability and achievement is based. It can influence whether a group has a high or a low average score but it does not influence how well individuals perform in relation to each other. This is where genes really matter, and this is where the biggest differences exist.

These are important issues, not least at a time when the world is working hard to bring education to every child. Under UNESCO's leadership most countries have committed to achieving universal enrolment in primary education by 2015, and in many countries the commitment is to make enrolment compulsory rather than optional. As a combined result of population growth and the proliferation of compulsory education, UNESCO estimates that over the next 30 years more people will receive a formal education than in the entirety of human history. Even though the 2015 target looks unlikely to be met in full this is a remarkable, wonderful achievement, and those who have found ways to bring educational opportunity to children of all backgrounds, in distant, poor, rural locations where the obstacles must seem insurmountable deserve the world's admiration and appreciation. But this advent of universal education has to come with an acceptance that by creating equal educational opportunities we put nature, in the form of genetic inheritance, back in the driving seat. By providing education to all children we create a situation in which their genes are the single biggest influence on how well, relative to others, they do in school. Universal education increases average performance but also highlights individual differences. This, if the first aim of education is genuinely met, seems, at worst, a small price to pay. At best, it offers the chance to select the best color and texture of icing for each and every child's educational cake. It allows schools to help their pupils become the best that they can be.

The school system has a responsibility to equip young people with the tools they need to live independently in society; there will also be social and economic benefits to developing a workforce and a citizenry with close to 100% literacy, numeracy, and understanding of digital technologies. Arguably, education could stop there. However, in a country with the resources and the will to take it further, the fact of genetically influenced individual differences begins to come into play for everyone, not just those who struggled to fill their basic toolkits. Once pupils have been equipped with the basic skills they need to function effectively in the world, the focus must switch to drawing out individual potential. In this way schools can promote individual fulfillment and achievement, and prepare cohorts of young people who know their talents and have been educated to use them. Society will surely benefit from generation after generation of young people with a firm grasp of core skills underpinning a wide range of specialist abilities and interests. We would predict positive impacts on health, law and order, employment, and the economy.

Diverse Opportunities to Draw Out Individual Potential

Everyone knows that some children have an aptitude and a taste for traditional academic work. Both qualities are influenced – but not determined – by genes. These pupils are the easiest for schools to handle, and they tend to do well in the current system. They are also the pupils that selective schools pick out and whose successes are then claimed by the schools to be the result of a superior education. Current policies and the "blank slate" philosophy hold up these children as models. They suggest that if we work harder then all children can be made to fit this mold. As a result, current approaches push nonacademic children to become mediocre generalists regardless of their natural abilities, interests, hopes, and dreams. This is one of the ways in which current educational policies and practices need to be changed – and genetics can suggest changes that might have a positive impact.

A society that recognizes and rewards a wide variety of skills and talents is likely to reap benefits. As children we are taught that the loops, swirls, and whorls on our fingertips make us unique; for most children this knowledge is a source of wonder and delight. Uniqueness *is* wonderful and delightful. But the current education system too often tries to suppress this uniqueness and turn out young people who are the same as everyone else. Square pegs in round holes. Even the most basic understanding of genetics tells us that schools would serve their pupils – and society – better by developing their unique talents and interests; by finding methods of teaching that allow Sam to be Sam and Sarah to be Sarah and help both of them to become fully functioning citizens of the worlds they choose to inhabit. A more detailed understanding of the way that genes and environments interact suggests that breadth of choice is the key – and we'll explain why later in the book.

In other words, once the basics have been instilled, a higher-level purpose of education should be to draw out the potential within a child and to support each child by nurturing that potential. This "drawing out" is the meaning of the Latin *educere*, from which the word education is derived. Enabling a child to recognize his or her abilities and to develop a love of learning is a powerful responsibility and will call upon all of the intelligence, sensitivity, and expert knowledge that the best teachers have. Teachers need to be experts in child development too, with strong personal and communication skills that allow them to connect with individual pupils, understand their needs and desires, and nurture them in the appropriate way. It helps when teaching is a respected profession and when teacher training is competitive and attracts large numbers of high-caliber graduates. It helps, too, when these high-caliber teachers are trusted to get on with teaching in the way that works best for them and their students.

DNA in the Classroom

What we have described above is a system of personalized learning – one that develops basic skills but also draws out and nurtures individual talents and abilities. The genetics of behavior can inform our thinking about how to make such a system a reality (skip to Chapters 13 and 14 if you want to see us try). The key is understanding the interplay between DNA (your genetic make-up or genotype) and the learning environment. In particular, we will draw on our knowledge of a process called genotype–environment correlation. There are three main types of correlation to note. The first is a *passive* genotype–environment correlation. This is the process whereby, for example, low-achieving parents with low aspirations pass on not only their genes but also an educationally unstimulating rearing environment to their children. Secondly, there is an *evocative* genotype–environment correlation. This is where children evoke certain behaviors on the basis of their genetic propensities. It is easy to see how this could be an important feature of personalized learning. If a teacher sees that a child is naturally quick with numbers they may offer more opportunities to that child to develop their mathematical skills and knowledge and keep pushing them forward regardless of what is expected of them on the basis of age alone. The same could be true for a fast runner, a child who is gifted with words, or a child with strong leadership or interpersonal skills. Teachers with the sensitivity (and time) to notice the strengths – and weaknesses – within an individual child, and to respond accordingly, offer those children an excellent chance of fulfilling their natural potential. Thirdly, there are *active* genotype–environment correlations. Here, children actively seek out experiences and opportunities on the basis of their genetic propensities. They are naturally drawn to the people and activities that suit them. In a classroom offering genuinely personalized learning children would be free to do this – like plants reaching for sun and water – and they would not be expected to put these urges to one side in order to conform to a rigorously planned timetable, apart from those lessons focused on teaching the essential basic skills.

Research into all three types of genotype–environment correlation shows us that sensitivity to genetically influenced differences between children represents the most promising means available to schools and teachers who wish to offer a genuinely personalized education. As well as sufficiently sensitive and skilled teaching and a classroom designed to foster creativity and personal development, the key to making this work is an understanding of genetics and the degree to which different behaviors are inherited. To this end genetics education should form a core part of all teacher training.

In Summary . . .

The primary aim of education is to furnish each and every child with a basic toolkit of literacy, numeracy, and technological skills, to the benefit of the children themselves and society at large. Any education system that allows a child to leave school without these skills has failed. Genetics tells us that some children will, by their very nature, find the acquisition of these basic skills difficult and that they should be provided with personalized support to whatever extent is necessary to enable them to acquire an adequate toolkit of skills. Where education goes beyond this basic training it needs to accept and embrace pupils' individual differences, recognizing that they are not blank slates. By personalizing education, schools, through embracing the process of genotype–environment correlation, should draw out natural ability and build individual education plans for every single child, based on pupils' specific abilities and interests rather than on arbitrary hoops set in place by partisan, vote-courting governments.

Geneticists can help make these educational aims more achievable. Our evidence makes it crystal clear that treating children as blank slates or empty vessels, using a factory model of school-ing, and arbitrarily imposing the same targets for everyone are approaches that work against, rather than with, natural child development. Our schools and our educational policies will be improved if they are designed to respond to naturally occurring individual differences in ability and development. This is what the best teachers already try to do in their classrooms: thousands of teachers have told us that they know nature is at least as important an influence as nurture on ability and achievement (Walker and Plomin, 2005). However, great swathes of education policy mili-tate against taking genetics into account, fostering herding methods and making personalization virtually impossible.

As we said at the beginning, it's time for this situation to change. It's time for geneticists to sit down with educationalists and policy makers. It's the right time because we now know just about enough to begin to make a positive difference. We also need to be prepared for the genetic advances that are just round the corner. The technology will soon be available, for example, to use DNA "chips" to predict strengths and weaknesses for individual pupils and to use this information to put personalized strategies in place for them. The same technology is already used in heart medicine and immunology; it's only a matter of time before it can be adapted for education. But even harnessing the current power of behavioral genetics will undoubtedly improve the way we educate our children. In Part One of this book, we will present the evidence for that claim, and in Part Two we will make tentative suggestions – tentative because they need to be tested and an evidence base established before they become formal policy recommendations – for making it a reality. In the next chapter we'll start by explaining how behavioral geneticists know what they know.

References

OECD (2010). *The High Cost of Low Educational Performance: The Long-run Economic Impact of Improving PISA Outcomes.* Paris: OECD. DOI: 10.1787/9789264077485-en.

Walker, S.O. and Plomin, R. (2005). The Nature–Nurture question: Teachers' perceptions of how genes and the environment influence educationally relevant behavior. *Educational Psychology*, 25, 509–516. DOI: 10.1080/01443410500046697.

Further Reading

Collins, Francis (2010). *The Language of Life: DNA and the Revolution in Personalized Medicine*. New York: HarperCollins Publishers. Provides a first-rate and highly readable account of developments and precedents in personalized medicine.

Pinker, Steven (2002). *The Blank Slate: The Modern Denial of Human Nature*. New York: Penguin Putnam Inc. An important and entertaining discussion of why humans can no longer be viewed as "blank slates," and why they ever were.

Chapter 2

How We Know
What We Know

We are psychologists and behavioral geneticists working on the Twins' Early Development Study (TEDS).[1] All of the twins born in the England and Wales between 1994 and 1996 were invited to join TEDS, and we have been following the thousands of pairs whose parents chose to sign up ever since. These families make TEDS' contribution to an ongoing international effort to untangle genetic and environmental influences on learning possible. We are forever grateful to them for their support.

Our building houses a large basement laboratory where scientists, mainly biologists and biochemists, work with genetic material at a molecular level. The remaining three floors of the building are populated by psychologists, medics, epidemiologists, bioinformaticians, statisticians, project managers, data managers, and a wide range of support staff. Some teams use samples of twins; others

[1] Robert set up TEDS at the SGDP Centre, King's College London almost two decades ago, and Kathryn has been a researcher and collaborator on the study since 2000.

G is for Genes: The Impact of Genetics on Education and Achievement, First Edition.
Kathryn Asbury and Robert Plomin.
© 2014 John Wiley & Sons, Inc. Published 2014 by John Wiley & Sons, Inc.

adoptees and their families; some the children of twins; and still others stepfamilies. Our studies can involve bringing participants into the center to observe and test them; communicating using telephones and the Internet; or going to families' homes. Sometimes we just talk to the participants in our studies, sometimes we test what they can do, and sometimes we take samples of their DNA or ask them to take part in neuroimaging studies. Everybody in our building, and everything we do, is aimed at gaining a better understanding of the workings of nature and nurture and the interplay between them.

In this chapter we focus briefly on how twin studies work, partly because our own research uses twins and partly because it is the research design that has been used most commonly around the world in genetically sensitive educational research. We also describe game-changing developments in DNA sequencing. We hope that this background information will give you a sense of how we arrived at the findings described in the rest of this book, and the possibilities for future developments combining techniques drawn from both genetics and education.

Twins: A Natural Experiment

The twin study is the most popular research design in behavioral genetics. By studying the differences between identical and non-identical twins it is possible to untangle nature and nurture in a way that is meaningful for all of us. Over the last 18 years the TEDS twins and their families have generously provided us with the information that underpins many of the research findings and ideas we discuss in this book. So, what is it about twins that make them so interesting to geneticists?

Well, the basic answer is that identical (monozygotic; MZ) twins share 100% of their genes, whereas fraternal (dizygotic; DZ) twins share 50% of their genes. Twins are a unique and important natural experiment. By measuring whether MZ twins are more similar than DZ twins on any human behavioral trait we can estimate the degree to which that trait is influenced by genes. We use twins to estimate how much of the difference between people on traits ranging from obesity to psychopathy to academic achievement is due to genetic influence (heritability); how much to shared environmental effects arising from, say, a shared home and family environment (traditional nurture); and how much to the effects of unique experiences not shared with others in the family, such as accidents, friendships and good old-fashioned lucky breaks.

We calculate the heritability of a particular behavior by comparing how similar identical twins are with how similar nonidentical twins are. If MZ twins are more similar than DZ twins we accept this as evidence of genetic influence, because the defining difference between the two groups is the fact that that identical twins are genetically more alike than nonidentical twins. We use correlation to define similarity. If twins correlate 1.00 we can deduce that there are no differences between them; they are exactly the same as each other. If they correlate 0.00 we can deduce that there are no similarities. Understandably the actual correlation almost always falls somewhere between these two extremes. If MZ twins correlate 0.75 on a particular behavior, say shyness, and DZ twins correlate 0.50, we double the difference between the two correlations (2×0.25) and estimate the heritability of shyness as 50%. This leaves the remaining 50% to be explained by the environment that children are growing up in.

Behavioral geneticists divide nurture or environment into two chunks. We call the first "shared environment" (SE) and the second "nonshared environment" (NSE). Shared environment represents nongenetic influences that affect children growing up in the same family in the same way. These might include the shared effects of a particular home or neighborhood, school, diet, access to TV or the Internet, pocket money, parents' relationship, parents' education, family income, a piano or books in the home, or a shared family pet. Anything that exists for both twins in a pair (or for non-twin siblings growing up together), and is experienced in the same way by them, is a shared environmental influence. This is the branch of nurture that has typically been credited with either making us great or screwing us up. For a wonderful account of the evidence against this Philip Larkinesque world view ("They fuck you up, your mum and dad") see *The Nurture Assumption* by Judith Rich Harris (Harris, 1999). Harris argues that, apart from passing on their genes, parents have little effect on how their children turn out. Their impact is largely restricted to the quality of their relationship with their children, and of the children's memories of growing up. She claims that peers rather than parents are likely to be a stronger environmental influence on the way that children develop into adults. The peers hypothesis awaits further proof, but a growing body of research confirms that the environments that cause differences between us are those that are not experienced in the same way by siblings growing up together.

The difference between the MZ correlation and 1.00 represents our estimate of nonshared environmental influence (NSE), experiences that are unique to the individual. Experiences can be objectively nonshared, that is, one twin could slip on ice and break a leg whereas the other does not. One could get the last available spot in the school swim team on a day when the other is at home with flu. They could choose or be chosen by different best friends, be in different classes or, individually, be in the right or wrong place at the right or wrong time. Over the years nonshared experiences small and large will contribute to making identical twins into increasingly different people. The same set of DNA travels along two divergent paths of experience, making identical twins ever more different as a result. Perceived or subjective nonshared environment is also recognized as important to development. So, for example, if the parents of twins divorce it is possible, perhaps even likely, that the two children will experience that divorce differently from each other, even if they are identical twins. One may have been closer to the parent who is leaving the family home; one may have overheard a particularly nasty argument; one may be more sensitive to change than the other or be going through a difficult experience at school at the same time. In this way an objectively shared event is transformed into a nonshared experience; the same divorce is different for each child. Later in the book we will describe studies that show that identical twins do, in fact, perceive the world differently from each other. In particular, in Chapter 9 we will show that they experience school differently, even when they are in the same class and are taught by the same teacher.

In summary, we use evidence from twins to estimate the relative influences of genes, shared, and nonshared environment on the differences between people on any given trait. Once we have this information we can search for the actual genes and the actual experiences involved, always aiming to learn how to use them to maximize individual potential and fulfillment. We have had sufficient success in this regard to begin to develop an understanding of how to use individualized genetic and environmental information to help all children to learn as effectively as possible.

DNA Sequencing

Once upon a time everybody thought that if we could just unravel our DNA and get a really good, close look at it we would be able to find the gene for math, the gene for writing, the gene for long legs, and the gene for a dazzling white smile. Well, the genome has been sequenced now and that's not quite how things have played out. What has emerged from molecular genetics is that most human attributes are influenced by a combination of many genes, and that the individual genes involved each have a small effect, making them exceedingly difficult to find. In spite of this unforeseen challenge, progress is still being made towards identifying genes that influence learning ability and school achievement, and new technology that will make progress even faster is emerging. The most exciting new directions ahead of us involve learning to use the new tools of molecular genetics to identify the genes that influence learning abilities and learning difficulties, and harnessing the results of this research to make a positive, practical difference to education.

The Human Genome Project was completed in 2003, exactly 50 years after the discovery of the structure and function of DNA (Watson and Crick, 1953). It required the effort of 2000 researchers and cost $3 billion. It stands as testimony to the speed of technological innovation in molecular genetics that one decade later we can now sequence the genome of an individual in just a few hours for less than $20,000. It is expected that the cost will decrease even further, to less than $10,000, within just a few years. As the technology advances, whole-genome sequencing will become ever-faster and ever more affordable, and in doing so will have a monumental impact on the world.

As the cost of DNA sequencing continues to plummet we will enter an era in which the entire sequence of the genome will be known for many individuals, raising new questions about who we are and how we live as individuals and as a species. Some members of the genomics community have predicted that whole-genome sequencing will be a standard part of medicine in the next few years. For instance Francis Collins, Director of the US National Institutes of Health, and former Director of the Human Genome Project, has written: "I am almost certain... that whole-genome sequencing will become part of newborn screening in the next few years... It is likely that within a few decades people will look back on our current circumstances with a sense of disbelief that we screened for so few conditions."(Collins, 2010, p. 50.) Such screening is not yet possible but Collins' prediction is a realistic one. Its implications – practical, ethical, moral, legal, political, and educational – are immense and merit serious consideration.

In the meantime, while the cost of whole-genome sequencing is still relatively prohibitive, researchers use DNA arrays ("gene chips"), tiny devices capable of genotyping one million DNA variants at a time. These allow us to focus on the bits of DNA that vary between us. All of humanity shares 95% of its DNA (to put this into context we also share more than half of our DNA with bananas). The remaining 5% lies at the heart of behavioral genetics and explains the heritability of differences between people. DNA arrays became commercially available in 2000 and can genotype millions of DNA variants quickly and inexpensively. One of the many strengths of "gene chips" is that they can be customized. We already have CardioChip, a microarray for DNA variants known to be related to cardiovascular function; and ImmunoChip for immunological dysfunction. Eventually we will have a Learning Chip, a reliable genetic predictor of the heritable differences between children in terms of their cognitive ability and academic achievement. How would we want to use such a chip? What advantages and what potentially problematic issues would its existence create? It's time to start asking – and answering – these questions, and we will begin to do so in Chapter 14, although a huge amount of scientific and public debate is needed to resolve them responsibly. Specialist DNA arrays are expensive to produce, but they could prove highly cost-effective if researchers and policy makers collaborated in finding ways to use them to design genetically sensitive interventions that could support at-risk children, perhaps to the extent of preventing some learning problems from ever emerging.

In the last few years genome-wide association studies have revolutionized our attempts to find the DNA variation responsible for the heritability of a wide range of medical conditions, educational outcomes, and common behavioral traits (Hirschhorn and Daly, 2005). Because common human traits are now accepted to be influenced by many genes, each of small effect, the capacity to scan the entire genome for any or all DNA variants associated with them has facilitated huge leaps forward in genetic research. It will almost certainly speed up the process of applying basic science to aspects of everyday life including education. We need to be ready for the changes that lie ahead.

References

Collins, Francis (2010). *The Language of Life: DNA and the Revolution in Personalized Medicine*. New York: HarperCollins Publishers.

Harris, J.R. (1999). *The Nurture Assumption: Why Children Turn Out the Way they Do*. New York: Touchstone.

Hirschhorn, J.N. and Daly, M.J. (2005). Genome-wide association studies for common diseases and complex traits. *Nature Reviews Genetics*, 6, 95–108.

Watson, J.D. and Crick, F.H.C. (1953). Genetical implications of the structure of deoxyribonucleic acid. *Nature*, 171, 964–967.

Further Reading

Plomin, R. (2008). *State-of-Science Review: SR-D7 – Genetics and the Future Diagnosis of Learning Disabilities. Review commissioned as part of UK Government's Foresight Project, Mental Capital and Wellbeing.* London: Government Office for Science. A discussion of the potential for using genetic information to predict and prevent common learning difficulties.

Plomin, R. (2013). Child development and molecular genetics: 14 years later. *Child Development*, 84(1), 104–20. DOI: 10.1111/j.1467-8624 .2012.01757.x. An account of the progress made – and the problems encountered – in identifying and using genes in developmental research and how this differs from what we expected.

Plomin, R. and Schalkwyk, L.C. (2007). Microarrays. *Developmental Science*, 10, 19–23. For further information about "gene chips."

Plomin, R., DeFries, J.C., Knopik, V.S., and Neiderhiser, J.M. (2013). *Behavioral Genetics* 6th ed. New York: Worth. The leading textbook in behavioral genetics. The sixth edition provides an up-to-date account of developments in the field.

Trouton, A., Spinath, F.M., and Plomin, R. (2002). Twins Early Development Study (TEDS): A multivariate, longitudinal genetic investigation of language, cognition, and behavior problems in childhood. *Twin Research*, 5, 444–448. A description of the TEDS sample and study.

http://www.genome.gov/11006943. For more information regarding the Human Genome Project (accessed 17 June 2013).

Chapter 3

The 3Rs: Reading, wRiting . . .

Watching young children learn to read is magical. Witnessing them gradually decode the unfamiliar symbols on the page in front of them and, over time, put them together and transform them into the stories and information that they represent is a moving experience for a parent. The first time your child pads up behind you as you sit "working" at your computer and haltingly sounds out "Amazon" or "Google" you overflow with pride and sheer wonder. How did they do it? How did they ever figure it out? (Can they tell you're not really working?) Watching them concentrate, eyebrows furrowed, as they pick up a book and read alone for pleasure for the first time is inspiring. We see through new eyes an activity that most of us conduct on automatic pilot. It's like watching them hop into the car, find biting point, check the rear view mirror, and drive off down the road . . . except more impressive (most of us would find driving lessons easier than a course of advanced code-cracking, which is what learning to read involves).

We like to think of ourselves as a highly evolved species, but one of the most interesting facts about reading is that it is too recent a development in our evolutionary history to be innate. We are not born with a reading instinct; if we were not taught, we would never learn to read. Reading is an environmentally triggered skill, which natural selection may well favor over time, but it is not a part of our nature. And yet our research shows that genes can in large part account for the differences between children in how well they can read. How can this be? How can evolutionary theory predict that reading ability (or disability) is not genetic when behavioral genetic research tells us that it is? To solve the conundrum, you need to consider the combination of skills that help us to learn to read. The following factors are all implicated (but not all are necessary, as the fact that blind and deaf children can become highly skilled readers amply demonstrates).

We need the ability to see and the ability to hear, as our earliest teachers point to letters and tell us how they sound. We need to be able to make a mental link between sounds (phonemes) and their physical presentation on the page (graphemes). Once we can recognize individual sounds we must learn how to blend them. When we can blend sufficiently well we need to comprehend what the sounds grouped into words and sentences actually mean so that f-l-o-w-e-r connects with our visual sense and our imagination to create a mental image of something with petals and a stem. In some young minds the flower will be a daisy, in others a rose, in some a line drawing, in others a photograph or a memory. But the graphemes and phonemes involved in f-l-o-w-e-r should, in the mind of a child who has learnt to read them, inspire a flower to grow.

To see, to hear, to make connections, and to imagine. Reading is not the primary purpose of any of these skills. They are naturally occurring abilities, shaped by life experiences, which are important to survival. Rather, reading is a social construct that puts these abilities to an amazing and innovative new use, like putting wood and friction together and creating fire. That is why reading is heritable, because it is an ability of many parts, most of which are subject to some genetic influence. And it is also the reason why labeling and solving the problems that some children and adults have with learning to read is particularly difficult. Is the obstacle to be found in the visual system, the auditory system, neural circuitry, cognitive building blocks, DNA, personality, the home environment, the school environment, all of the above, or somewhere else instead?

From DNA to ABC

Reading is the academic ability that has received most attention from behavioral genetic researchers (Olson, 2007). This is partly because it is easier to measure than some other abilities but also because reading is something of a sacred cow in our culture. A child who struggles with science, sport, history, music, or even mathematics tends not to inspire the same panic as a child who struggles with learning to read, although there are some documented cultural differences in this regard. Adults in some countries, for instance, would feel just as embarrassed about having to admit they were not good with numbers as they would about admitting they couldn't read very well.

Reading ability is distributed normally – a classic bell curve. That is, most people cluster around average ability, with a small proportion excelling and a small proportion struggling. Our ability to read is heavily influenced by our genes: estimates of heritability tend to hover between 60 and 80%. This means that a significant proportion of the differences between individuals in how well they can read can be explained by genetic influence, leaving as little as 20% to be explained by the environment in some studies (Kovas, Haworth, Dale, and Plomin, 2007; Wilcutt et al., 2010). Similar results have recently been reported from China, in spite of the very different orthography of Chinese (Chow et al., 2011).

Researchers have also begun to find particular genes which might be associated with reading ability, but even if these findings are replicated each of them can only account for a tiny proportion of the differences between people in how well they can read.

This well-documented pattern ties in with something known as the Quantitative Trait Loci (QTL) hypothesis, which is based on a huge amount of supporting data. The QTL hypothesis proposes that, apart from a group of mainly rare and severe single-gene disorders, all common human traits are influenced by many genes and each gene has only a tiny effect. This is different from what we originally expected and very different from what the press often reports. It means there is not, and will never be, a single language gene, ADHD gene, cancer gene, or football gene. The genes that influence most of what we do are common variants rather than rare mutations. They are carried by great swathes of the population, by people at every point on the normal distribution. They combine to influence our thoughts, our behavior, and how society labels us. Rich man, poor man, beggar man, thief? Dyslexic, gifted, antisocial, shy? Together, in concert with each other and with environmental influences, they position people on a continuous spectrum of whatever human trait is being measured, a bell curve of ability, health, or happiness.

One major consequence of this is that we begin to see the abnormal as normal. That is, those at the extremes of ability, health, and happiness (the "abnormal") are not usually genetically distinct from everybody else. People with mild learning difficulties and physical or mental health problems are usually on the same bell curve as everyone else, and are usually affected by the same genes as everyone else too. What has commonly been referred to as disorder or disability (abnormality) is usually just the low-ability end of the normal distribution.

This is not true for devastating and rare single-gene disorders such as Huntington's disease or Rett syndrome, or for genetic or chromosomal learning difficulties, which render the people who suffer from them statistical outliers. These people are genetically distinct from the general population in real and often difficult ways. But for common human traits it is usually inaccurate to say that some people have a genetic disorder while the rest of us are "normal" and fine. An ever-growing mountain of research consistently finds that this is simply not the case. Most human traits – including reading (Fisher and DeFries, 2002) – are influenced by many genes

(QTL hypothesis) and many experiences, and people with problems are influenced by the same genes as everybody else. The abnormal is normal. Most of what we do can be placed on a continuum of human behavior, making our behavior relative to, rather than distinct from, that of other people. As we will see in Part Two of this book, this has major implications for the way the education system should be constructed.

* * * * *

Much behavioral research into the genetics of reading has derived from four major twin studies with samples drawn from Australia, Scandinavia, the United Kingdom, and the United States. This means that we are in a position to comment on the genetic and environmental influences on reading ability in these populations. What the studies tend to find, apart from moderate to strong heritability estimates, is that reading shows strong genetic stability. That is, the relevant genes are switched on early in childhood and appear to remain active throughout the lifespan. For example, it has been found that pre-reading skills, such as learning the alphabet, correlate genetically with reading skills years later (Hayiou-Thomas, Harlaar, Dale, and Plomin, 2006; Hensler, Schatschneider, Taylor, and Wagner, 2010). In other words, the genes influencing little Tommy's impressive grasp of his ABCs at age 3 will still influence his reading of Harry Potter at age 9.

This finding ties in with one of the major principles unearthed by behavioral genetic research, namely that continuity is genetic and change is environmental. Any large, uncharacteristic fluctuation in performance over time, in either direction, is likely to be the result of experience rather than genes – think inspirational teacher, extensive practice, traumatic loss, or bad company. This maxim, that continuity is genetic and change is environmental, forms one of the cornerstones of our ideas regarding genetically sensitive education. We will be building on it in Part Two of the book.

However, it is in many ways too simplistic to say that reading is 60 or 70% heritable. We are all different and that is partly because our genes are different. Genetic variation exists from the moment we are born, but is multiplied and magnified as our genes interact with each other and with our environment. It is likely that some environmental effects are hidden within our heritability estimates because they are effective indirectly, via their interplay with genes.

A good example of gene–environment interplay, although not the type that behavioral geneticists usually study, was found in an important and ongoing twin study of reading which recruited twins from three continents, North America (Colorado), Europe (Norway and Sweden), and Australia (New South Wales) (Samuelsson et al., 2008). Behavioral genetics is normally the study of differences between individuals rather than between groups. However, this research is pertinent to debates about raising the average ability of an entire state or nation. Children from Colorado and Australia are required by law to attend school from the age of 5. However, whereas the Australian children go to school from 9 a.m. to 3 p.m. 5 days a week, the American children only attend their kindergartens for 3 or 4 hours each day. Furthermore the Australian children's education is regulated by a state-wide curriculum mandating that at least 35% of the week should be devoted to language and literacy instruction. There is no state-mandated curriculum for teaching reading and spelling in Colorado.

An even more striking comparison emerges with the introduction of the children from Sweden and Norway. In these countries compulsory schooling begins when children are 7 years old. In practice almost all children attend kindergarten before this but the emphasis in kindergarten is on social, emotional, and aesthetic development rather than learning to read. If children can read before they begin school it is because they learn at home, suggesting that shared environmental influences (those shared by children growing up in the same family) on reading ability may be more important to these Scandinavian twins than to their American and Australian counterparts. Once children begin First Grade at age 7 in Sweden and Norway, reading and spelling are the primary target activities in school, and literacy instruction is guided by a master plan common to all schools across the two countries.

So, what did these population differences in experience mean for the heritability of reading ability in kindergarten and First Grade? What would your hypothesis be? Should the relative influence of nature and nurture differ across countries? And in what ways? Take a few moments to think about it before you move on.

Well, what the researchers actually found was that the pattern of genetic and environmental influence did indeed differ across countries. At the end of kindergarten about 80% of individual differences between the Australian children could be accounted for by their genes, with the remaining 20% divided pretty equally between shared and nonshared environmental influence. By comparison, genes explained two-thirds of the differences between the Colorado children, with most of the remainder explained by nonshared environment. Finally, differences between the Scandinavian children, who had not experienced any reading instruction at all in school, showed far less genetic influence. Genes accounted for only one-third of the differences between these children at the end of kindergarten. So, where the heritability estimate was close to 80% for the Australian it was closer to 30% for the Scandinavian children. By stark contrast to the North American and Australian children, around half of the observed reading differences were accounted for by shared environmental – probably family – influence.

So, by the end of kindergarten, genes had most impact on the children with most schooling. Also, illiteracy rates were much higher in the Scandinavian countries than in Australia. But, then look at what happens by the end of First Grade, when all children have experienced intensive literacy teaching. By the end of First Grade, genes explained around 80% of the differences between children not just in Australia but in all three samples. Shared environment explained next to nothing in any of the countries and nonshared environment explained 10 to 20%. Literacy rates were roughly equivalent in all three groups. It is counterintuitive. More school – that is, more environmental input – leads to greater genetic influence rather than greater environmental influence. So what's going on?

Well, as we discussed in Chapter 1, universal education is likely to lead to increased heritability estimates, and that's precisely what we see happening here. As children's experiences become more similar they start to explain and increase the similarities between them rather than the differences. Therefore genetic influence, relatively speaking, becomes stronger. In this instance major differences in access to formal reading instruction disappear by the end of First Grade and can no longer explain differences in reading ability between pupils. Average reading ability increases as a direct result of this but at the same time the heritability of reading also increases. If environmental factors cannot explain differences between people it is because they have been equalized – all pupils have been given a similar opportunity to learn. In this sense a case can be made that heritability estimates act as an index of equality. A large heritability estimate does not indicate that the environment has no influence, just that it influences similarities rather than differences. This study represents a wonderful example of how even very high levels of genetic influence on a trait do not make the environment, in this case formal instruction in schools, redundant. On the contrary, schools are the reason children across the three continents learnt to read. Genes, however, are the primary reason why some of them are better readers than others.

The important point here for schools is that we can raise average performance, and all children will benefit, by the application of good, universal educational interventions. This supports the current push for more experimental trials of what really works in education. At the beginning of the 19th century more than 50% of most Western populations were illiterate. However, at this time lack of education was a much better predictor of illiteracy than genetically influenced low ability. A behavioral genetic analysis of data from that time would, if it were possible to perform, show strong environmental but weak genetic influences on individual differences in reading ability. The introduction of compulsory education for all changed that. When all children are offered education the differences between them are primarily caused by individual differences in their response to instruction. A good educational intervention targeted at every child in a country will boost the national average, and probably the heritability of the skill that has been targeted, but it will not do much to close the gap between the most and least able learners. The implications of this for supporting struggling learners are important.

Another point to consider is that although there were high rates of illiteracy at the end of kindergarten in Norway and Sweden, pupils from these countries are known to go on to become better than average readers. This indicates that, if delaying formal instruction can be shown to be better for children's welfare and overall development, we can hypothesize that it is unlikely to cause long-term damage to their reading skills. This, like all hypotheses, would require formal scientific testing before being implemented as a national policy. However, as an evidence-based hypothesis it has merit.

Genes, and therefore human potential, cannot grow in a vacuum. Heritability estimates are not as straightforward as they first appear because they are subject to the fundamental interdependence of genes and experience. It is all very well to say that reading ability is 60 or 70 or 80% heritable, but such a statement does not make the pivotal role of teaching apparent. Children with a genetic predisposition to be good at reading would not learn to read if they were not taught to do so, or at least exposed to lots of print. In this light, causing an increase in heritability (at the same time as an increase in skill) can reasonably be seen as an achievement of which teachers and parents should be proud, rather than a sign of determinism to be mistrusted and feared. If all children attended equally good schools and received an equally good education genes would account for most of the differences – and there would be almost as many as there are now – between them in terms of their reading ability. And that does not have to be a bad thing, especially if these schools push average performance up and shift the whole bell curve along to the right. A good school should provide equally good nurture for each child's nature. We don't all have the same talents but we should all have equal opportunities to develop the talents we have.

Environmental Influences on Reading Ability

There has been less genetically sensitive research into environmental influences on reading ability than we need. As we have seen, shared environmental influences appear to be important in the preschool years but environmental influences at school tend to be nonshared. Language and literacy in the home have been found time and time again to influence children's reading abilities (e.g. Mol and Bus, 2011). In studies that do not take genes into account socioeconomic status (SES) is often shown to predict reading ability. At three years of age, for example, children in the US Head Start program lag significantly behind their peers in terms of the size of their vocabulary (e.g. Scheffner-Hammer, Farkas, and Maczuga, 2010). Similar differences have been shown for reading in the primary-school years. So, children from low-income families where the parents have low levels of education appear to be at risk of becoming struggling readers.

Some argue that socioeconomic status (SES) – usually defined as the educational and occupational status of parents – affects ability via the quality of the linguistic environment provided in the home. For example, it has been shown that speaking directly to children, encouraging them to talk, and exposing them to a diverse and complex vocabulary are all linked to larger vocabularies in young children. On the face of it this is not exactly rocket science. Also, how responsive a mother is to her young child has been linked to expressive language skills including the timing of early milestones such as first words (e.g. Laranjo and Bernier, 2012). These practices are found less often, on average, in low SES homes. It is important to emphasize however that, even if we could take these findings as givens, there is in fact a great deal of variability at different levels of socioeconomic status. Some lower-status families, for example, provide outstanding literacy environments for their children while some high-status families offer their children little in the way of communication. Averages tell us little about individuals.

However, without taking genetics into account it is impossible to interpret findings such as these. We can't actually know that low SES is associated with low reading ability for environmental reasons. Do parents who don't talk to their children very much cause a lack of vivacious chat in their offspring or are their offspring uncommunicative because they are genetically similar to their parents? Or is there some combination of both factors at work? As is almost always the case with behavioral genetic findings, a combination of the two seems most likely.

Recent work has focused on genotype–environment correlations, a concept which describes how our genes influence our experiences and demonstrates the way that genes do not operate in a vacuum but play an active part in our experience. As discussed in Chapter 1, there are three types of genotype–environment correlation: passive, evocative, and active.

In a passive genotype–environment correlation we see the results of receiving our genes and our environments from the same parents. For example, parents who do not enjoy reading pass on their genes to their children, but they also create a home in which, perhaps, there are not many books, library trips, or bedtime stories. Therefore, the child is in a position where they may inherit genes that do not favor reading along with a home environment that is not conducive to developing a love of reading. A double whammy.

In an evocative genotype–environment correlation a child who is genetically predisposed towards a love of reading may evoke different behaviors from family and friends than a child who is not. They may be read stories, taken to the library and bought books as presents. They might be referred to as a bookworm, making a love of reading part of their identity, and they might be praised for the amount that they read or the speed at which they read it. This atmosphere of praise and positivity about the written word is partly evoked by the child's genes.

In an active genotype–environment correlation children who are genetically predisposed to be good at reading might volunteer to read the longest poem in the school assembly, and be noticed for doing it; they might spend free time in the library and discover that science fiction is their thing; or they might race through the reading schemes so quickly that they are given new, more challenging tasks in class and therefore offered a more personalized education than their classmates. In an active genotype–environment correlation people of all ages shape their own worlds on the basis of their genetically influenced propensities. As researchers, we believe this process is hugely important in education, but new methods for measuring, understanding, and making the most of it are required, something we are working hard on at the moment. In a genotype–environment correlation, genes, via personality, behavior, or ability, affect exposure to certain environments. We shape and create our own experiences.

The other major type of genotype–environment interplay that researchers have identified is gene (or genotype) × environment interaction, known as G×E. G×E exists if our genes can be shown to affect our susceptibility to certain environments. In the case of reading ability, we would see indicators of G×E interaction if reading ability were more (or less) heritable for groups of children (e.g. girls, children from low-income families, children identified as gifted or talented) who experienced a particular environment (say an intensive reading course) than for children in general. For example, in two studies of G×E in relation to reading it has been found that the heritability of word recognition is substantially higher among twins with highly educated parents than it is among children with less well-educated parents (Friend *et al.*, 2009). This may mean that better-educated parents provide an environment for their children in which genes are in the driver's seat when it comes to learning to read. This may reflect the finding described earlier that heritability increases as intensity of education increases and that better-educated parents give their children more education than others. Perhaps there is something specific about the environment that these parents provide that is especially effective in nurturing their children's natures. This is something to explore when considering how to equalize opportunities for all children, regardless of the family they are born into, the neighborhood in which they grow up, and the schools they attend. Interestingly, a similar pattern has been found in schools, with reading ability shown to be more heritable among students with better teachers (Taylor *et al.*, 2010) and less heritable among children growing up in low-income neighborhoods (Taylor and Schatschneider, 2010). A formal, biologically-based G×E interaction would involve finding that an environmental intervention, such as an intensive phonics course or shared book-reading, has significantly more impact on children carrying one version of a gene than on children carrying the alternative version. G×E of this type has been found in research into childhood maltreatment and aggression but has not yet been found in the field of reading research.

An understanding of the interplay between genotypes and environments can help teachers and policy makers to understand why some interventions and methods help some children and not others. G×E interactions can help decision makers to target resources more accurately and with greater confidence. The "what works" agenda needs to take individual differences into account by looking at what works for which children and in which circumstances. Providing the right educational environment for a particular child's genotype also means providing as broad a range of environments as possible – a consideration that will have perhaps surprising implications for the type of school system we recommend in Part Two.

Struggling Readers

Not all children learn to read in their first year or two at school, and some of these children grow into adults without ever becoming truly comfortable with reading. The most commonly cited reading disability is dyslexia. We would like to offer a clear and simple definition of dyslexia, but different sources give different definitions, none of which are universally accepted. Some academics, teachers, and politicians have declared it a myth, while others, normally those who have been diagnosed with "dyslexia" or are involved with representing "dyslexics" in the public arena, respond with anger. The controversy is especially aggravating and distressing for parents when education professionals are arguing over a label instead of providing the help and support that their child clearly needs. In fact, the question of whether dyslexia exists or not is the hottest potato there is in research in learning disabilities.

Putting a precise definition to one side, it is fair to say that children who are tested for dyslexia all have at least one thing in common: they all struggle with learning to read. They are the children on the left-hand tail of reading's bell curve. Research suggests that 5 to 10% of schoolchildren experience difficulties with reading. Most of these children display several (but rarely all) of the following characteristics: difficulty generating rhyming words or counting syllables in words (phonological awareness); difficulty hearing and manipulating sounds in words (phonemic awareness); difficulty distinguishing different sounds in words (phonological processing); and difficulty in learning the sounds of letters (phonics). Their oral reading can be slow and laborious and their comprehension can be poor, although this is often not the case. Struggling readers also often experience difficulties with oral and written language. They may have been late in learning to talk, have difficulty following directions, and have struggled to learn the alphabet, nursery rhymes, and songs. They may have difficulty putting ideas on paper and, although they may do well on weekly spelling tests at school, are likely to make many spelling mistakes in their daily work. The difficulties these children experience in school can have a negative knock-on effect on their confidence and mental wellbeing.

So is there any evidence to suggest that children with dyslexia are genetically different in any way? If so, that would help to provide that elusive definition for the condition. Research has shown that reading difficulties run in families (DeFries, Vogler, and LaBuda, 1986). Behavioral geneticists have in fact identified specific genes that may be linked with reading problems (Scerri *et al.*, 2011). In this respect, research into the genetics of reading is more advanced than research into the genetics of school achievement generally. However, it is important to emphasize that the research is at an early stage and many results not only fail to replicate but also contradict each other.

One candidate gene for reading problems is called KIAA0319 and resides on chromosome 6 (Paracchini *et al.*, 2006). It is relatively promising because it has been found to be associated with reading difficulties in three different samples in the United States and the United Kingdom and, in a world where false positives are rife, replication of findings in different and independent groups of people is the key to trusting positive results. The discovery of KIAA0319 by a team at Oxford University met with a fairly typical media fanfare. The *Daily Mail*'s headline read: "Dyslexia gene discovery could improve treatment for millions."

This headline is actually relatively restrained but, even so, the only word in it that should be used with any confidence is "could." An association with reading difficulties does not make KIAA0319 a "dyslexia gene" any more than an association between you and gym membership makes you lithe, lissom, and fighting fit. And the leap from biological finding to improving treatment for millions is so vast that seven-league boots would struggle to carry you there. But the truth of the "could" is interesting. And the fact that the result has been replicated is cause for further exploration.

We know that reading ability has a normal distribution and that, at the least sophisticated level, reading disability can be defined with an arbitrary cut-off at the 5th or 10th percentile of that distribution. So, to cut to the chase, is the KIAA0319 gene only expressed in children at the low end of the distribution? Or those with a dyslexia diagnosis? Dr Silvia Paracchini from the Oxford team pursuing the link between KIAA0319 and reading problems asked exactly this question and found that KIAA0319 is in fact distributed throughout the population (Paracchini *et al.*, 2008). We all have it, however weak or strong our literacy skills. It appears to be associated with reading ability as well as disability. Its effect on reading ability throughout the entire distribution is statistically significant but very, very small. This brings us back to the QTL hypothesis, discussed in Chapter 2 (common human traits are influenced by many genes and many environments, each with a tiny effect). The QTL hypothesis would predict that there would be no specific biological markers for reading problems and that those with a medical diagnosis such as "dyslexia" would be influenced by the same genes as those without. This is exactly what the Oxford team has found.

In time KIAA0319 could prove to be one of dozens, maybe even hundreds, of genes that are relevant to reading ability. What this means in practice is that we won't see reliable DNA testing kits for dyslexia any time soon. The least able readers in a class struggle with reading whether they are labeled as dyslexic or not, and their struggle is partly rooted in their DNA. Reading ability is distributed in a bell curve and there is no obvious cut-off at which a child should be recognized as having a reading disorder. This has major implications for how to identify and support struggling readers.

As we mentioned earlier, "dyslexia" is something of a hot potato, and statements such as this are likely to get us into trouble. We venture to ask why? As parents, why do we find it easier to say "my child is dyslexic" than to say "my child finds reading hard"? What does it say about our attitude to our children having weaknesses as well as strengths? And what does it say about society and education policy that we don't immediately offer extra support to any child whose teachers and parents agree finds it more difficult than most to learn to read? Instead we first insist, in many instances, on having such a child tested (or having their parents independently organize and pay for testing) to see if they meet certain criteria and can be "diagnosed" as dyslexic.

We appreciate that in later years a diagnosis or record of some kind is helpful in ensuring that individuals are treated fairly. For example, a job applicant who struggles with their reading might perform poorly on a psychometric test if it has to be completed in a certain time. Assuming that the job is not dependent on reading speed, it might be more reasonable to revise the time limit for such a candidate. After all, you wouldn't ask someone with impaired vision to take the test without glasses or contact lenses.

However, the fact is that there is no simple genetic basis for a diagnosis of a disability called "dyslexia." The fact that a child cannot read as well as we would expect is all the evidence that should be required for them to be offered extra support. The money spent on testing and diagnosis – and the time spent waiting for all of this – would be better spent on extra support for all children at the low end of the reading-ability spectrum. If enacted as early in a child's education as possible, this could improve their performance and close the gap between the most and least able readers in a class.

The Genetics of Writing Ability

The ability to write has been given less consideration by behavioral geneticists than the ability to read. Research has tended to find strong links between reading and writing skills, which in many ways is unsurprising; both are modes of language and communication. Writing is an essential life skill in the modern world. Even if we have no desire to write plays, poetry, novels, essays, or letters we still need to fill in forms, sign for packages, make shopping lists, answer texts, and so on. The need is even more striking for schoolchildren, who usually have to demonstrate in writing what they have learnt in their lessons. Writing is the primary mechanism for getting the kind of school grades that will create attractive opportunities for the rest of their lives. That said, like reading, writing is an unnatural skill that without intensive instruction we would never come to master. And even with intensive instruction it turns out that some children find it an incredibly difficult skill to acquire.

Most behavioral genetic work on the etiology of writing skills has focused on spelling, although it could be argued that spelling is more closely linked to reading than writing. In the first twin study of spelling, genes were found to account for just over half of the differences between 13-year-old children.

A study led by Dr Bonamy Oliver in TEDS explored the genetics of writing achievement using UK National Curriculum levels awarded to the TEDS twins when they were 7 years old (Oliver, Dale, and Plomin, 2007). Dr Oliver gathered teacher ratings of the children's achievement and used the twin method to figure out that genes accounted for two-thirds of the differences between individual children, shared environment only 7%, and nonshared environmental influence the rest. The pattern is noticeably similar to that for reading achievement. She also explored whether the same pattern of nature and nurture was true for the lowest-performing children and found that it was. Low writing ability was no more or less heritable than average or high writing ability.

As yet there has been no attempt to identify specific genes or environments associated with writing but this remains an important area for future research. Our least able writers face a barrier between themselves and their society that is unacceptable. Identifying experiences that can overcome a genetic predisposition to finding writing difficult is an important and worthwhile scientific and social goal.

For both reading and writing then, we have seen heritability estimates of over 60%, evidence that the same genes operate throughout the ability spectrum (the abnormal is normal), and evidence that the same genes remain operational as children grow (continuity is genetic and change is environmental). That's two of the three "R"s covered. But how does 'Rithmetic compare? In the next chapter, we look at whether there is genetic evidence for treating the third "R" differently in our new education system.

References

Chow, B.W.-Y., Ho, C.S.-H., Wong, S.W.-L., Waye, M.M.Y., and Bishop, D.V.M. (2011). Genetic and environmental influences on Chinese language and reading abilities. *PLoS One*, 6: e16640.

DeFries, J.C., Vogler, G.P., and LaBuda, M.C. (1986). Colorado Family Reading Study: An overview. In J.L. Fuller and E.C. Simnel (eds), *Perspectives in Behavior Genetics* (pp. 29–56). Hillsdale, NJ: Erlbaum.

Fisher, S.E. and DeFries, J.C. (2002). Developmental dyslexia: Genetic dissection of a complex cognitive trait. *Nature Reviews Neuroscience*, 3, 767–780.

Friend, A., DeFries, J.C., Olson, R.K., Pennington, B., Harlaar, N., Byrne, B., Samuelsson, S., Willcutt, E.G., Wadsworth, S.J., Corley, R., and Keenan, J.M. (2009). Heritability of high reading ability and its interaction with parental education. *Behavior Genetics*, 39, 427–436.

Hayiou-Thomas, M. E., Harlaar, N., Dale, P. S., and Plomin, R. (2006). Genetic and environmental mediation of the prediction from preschool language and nonverbal ability to 7-year reading. *Journal of Research in Reading*, 29(1), 50–74.

Hensler, B.S., Schatschneider, C., Taylor, J., and Wagner, R.K. (2010). Behavioral genetic approach to the study of dyslexia. *Journal of Developmental and Behavioral Pediatrics*, 31, 525–532.

Kovas, Y., Haworth, C.M.A., Dale, P.S., and Plomin, R. (2007). The genetic and environmental origins of learning abilities and disabilities in the early school years. *Monographs of the Society for Research in Child Development*, 72, 1–144.

Laranjo, I. and Bernier, A. (2012). Children's expressive language in early toddlerhood: links to prior maternal mind-mindedness. *Early Child Development and Care*, 72, 748–767.

Mol, S.E. and Bus, A.G. (2011). To read or not to read: A meta-analysis of print exposure from infancy to early adulthood. *Psychological Bulletin*, 137(2), 267–296.

Oliver, B.R., Dale, P.S., and Plomin, R. (2007). Writing and reading skills as assessed by teachers in 7-year-olds: A behavioural genetic approach. *Cognitive Development*, 22 (1), 77–95.

Olson, R.K. (2007). Introduction to the special issue on genes, environment and reading. *Reading and Writing*, 20, 1–11.

Paracchini, S., Thomas, A., Castro, S., Lai, C., Paramasivam, M., Wang, Y., and Monaco, A.P. (2006). The chromosome 6p22 haplotype associated with dyslexia reduces the expression of KIAA 0319, a novel gene involved in neuronal migration. *Human Molecular Genetics*, 15(10), 1659–1666.

Paracchini, S., Steer, C.D., Buckingham, L.L., Morris, A.P., Ring, S., Scerri, T., Stein, J., Pembrey, M.E., Ragoussis, J., Golding, J., and Monaco, A.P. (2008). Association of the KIAA0319 dyslexia susceptibility gene with reading skills in the general population. *American Journal of Psychiatry*, 165, 1576–1584.

Samuelsson, S., Byrne, B., Olson, R.K., Hulslander, J., Wadsworth, S., Corley, R., Willcutt, E.G. and DeFries, J.C. (2008). Response to early literacy instruction in the United States, Australia and Scandinavia: A behavioural-genetic analysis. *Learning and Individual Differences*, 18 (3), 289–295.

Scerri, T.S., Morris, A.P., Buckingham, L.L., Newbury, D.F., Miller, L.L., Monaco, A.P., Bishop, D.V.M., and Paracchini, S. (2011). DCDC2,

KIAA0319 and CMIP are associated with reading-related traits. *Biological Psychiatry*, 70, 237–245.

Scheffner-Hammer, C., Farkas, G., and Maczuga, S. (2010). The language and literacy development of Head Start children: A study using the Family and Child Experiences Survey Database. *Language, Speech and Hearing Services in Schools*, 41, 70–83.

Taylor, J., Roehrig, A.D., Hensler, B.S., Connor, C.M., and Schatschneider, C. (2010). Teacher quality moderates the genetic effects on early reading. *Science*, 328 (5977), 512–514.

Wilcutt, E.G., Pennington, B.F., Duncan, L., Smith, S.D., Keenan, J.M., Wadsworth, S., DeFries, J.C., and Olson, R.K. (2010). Understanding the complex etiologies of developmental disorders: Behavioral and molecular genetic approaches. *Journal of Developmental and Behavioral Pediatrics*, 31, 533–544.

Further Reading

Haworth, C.M.A., Davis, O.S.P., and Plomin, R. (2013). Twins Early Development Study (TEDS): A genetically sensitive investigation of cognitive and behavioral development from childhood to young adulthood. *Twin Research and Human Genetics*, 16, 117–125.

and we have shown that reading difficulties represent one end of a normally distributed bell curve, and that they are affected by the same genes as reading ability in general. Many parents would prefer to believe that they have a bright child who has a specific disability, than that he or she has low ability in mathematics or, perhaps more especially, in reading. "Disability" implies diagnosis, whereas "difficulty" describes a common problem. But more of that later ...

Much debate also centers on the different aspects of mathematics – for example calculating and algebra – and whether they are linked or separate from each other. For example, are the ingredients that make a good actuary the same as those that make a good architect? What does the child who can recite prime numbers to the edge of the numerical universe have in common with the child who can calculate the profit he will make from selling his football cards in the school playground? And, what can these genetic findings tell us about how to go about teaching those children?

Kovas designed and conducted a study to address these questions using 10-year-old twins drawn from TEDS. The twins' teachers gave each child a score on the three areas of numeracy that are covered by the UK national curriculum – using and applying mathematics; numbers and algebra; and shapes, space, and measures – and the twins' mathematical ability was also assessed directly using an online testing procedure. The questions Kovas looked at were these: Is mathematical ability heritable? Are the genetic and environmental influences on low mathematical ability the same as those in children of average or high ability? And, are different mathematical abilities subject to the same genetic and environmental influences? She explored these questions statistically and then passed her findings on to Sophia Docherty in the labs, who examined the twins' DNA for further answers. So what did Kovas and Docherty find?

Is mathematical ability heritable?

Yes it is. Kovas estimated the heritability of mathematical ability among 10-year-old children, as rated by their teachers, as about two-thirds. Shared environment accounted for 12% of the ability differences between children, and nonshared environment accounted for 24%. She had carried out a similar analysis when the TEDS twins were 7 years old and reached a very similar conclusion: teacher-assessed mathematics achievement was 68% heritable, with shared environment accounting for 9% and non-shared environment 22% of the differences between children. Similar results also emerged when the children were 9 years old. In this sample at least, which is representative of the wider UK population, a heritability estimate of 60 to 70% appears to be robust throughout the early school years. This mirrors our results for reading and writing.

This is what primary school teachers are dealing with. Genetic differences at this stage are more important to mathematics achievement than differences in family income, family Monopoly or Rummikub sessions, parental education, gender, or school quality. Yet teacher training does not take them into account. In one sense, a heritability estimate of 60 to 70% tells the teacher nothing at all about what is possible, or even to be expected, from any particular child, but it should confirm that, for partly biological reasons, all of the children in her class are starting from different points and therefore need to take different next steps to develop their understanding and their ability. It should tell her that her job is to gradually draw out each child's potential rather than aiming, as a class, at some arbitrary, externally imposed target. Teachers already know this, but their methods are too often challenged by a political will to defy nature. Some kids start with a biological advantage in mathematics. It is not unreasonable to propose that those kids will develop differently from those who do not share their advantage. Is it unreasonable for education to reflect this?

The discovery of genetic influence on mathematical achievement and ability has important implications for how we teach mathematics, in particular for how we personalize numerical education so that it draws out the best every child has to offer while not detracting from the areas in which they stand to gain more fulfillment and higher achievement. In his book on success, *Outliers*, Malcolm

Gladwell (Gladwell, 2008) argues that success – real, high-level success – takes 10,000 hours of practice. Why not give children high-quality mathematical education in quantities appropriate to their individual abilities, needs, and hopes, and use education to help them to put in 10,000 hours where it really counts for them? If your dream is to be an Olympic gymnast or to run your own graphic-design business, beauty parlor, or garage, then you will need a certain amount of mathematics education, the kind of mathematics that you will use day to day in the 21st century (and let's face it, that's quite a lot); and it might be good for your overall mental dexterity and creativity to go further than that. But you won't need as much (or at least the same type) as the kid who wants to work out how long it will take a rocket to get to Neptune and design the engine that could power that rocket. People differ in their mathematical ability, and two-thirds of the differences between them are influenced by their genes. We think that matters – and we will take it into account when we attempt our line drawing of a genetically sensitive education system in Part Two.

Are the genetic and environmental influences on low mathematical ability the same as those in children of average or high ability?

Mathematical ability, like reading ability, is distributed in a bell-shaped curve, with most people clustering around the average while a small group really struggle and a small group excel. Let's think about high ability first. Mathematics appears to be the most fertile academic field for breeding genius, particularly precocious genius. It is unlikely that Shakespeare could have penned *Hamlet* in his pre-teen years, yet young mathematicians can reach extraordinary heights without being hindered by their relative lack of time on the job.

In 1985 Ruth Lawrence was photographed in full academic regalia riding around Oxford University on the back of her father's tandem. At the ripe old age of 13 she graduated from Oxford with a starred first and a special commendation. She had completed her degree in two rather than the standard three years. She subsequently completed a PhD, went to Harvard and from there to the University of Michigan to study knot theory. Lawrence is now a mathematics professor at the Einstein Institute of Mathematics in Israel (one can only assume Albert would not be pleased to have a mathematics institute named after him). She obviously is and always was good at math. Very good to be fair. Perhaps even a genius. Her mathematical ability, like everyone else's, is partly rooted in her genes but it is likely that her unusual rearing environment also played a part.

Lawrence was home-schooled by her father (it turns out most mathematics prodigies are home-schooled), she barely left her father's side at Oxford (he attended lectures with her but was eventually banned from the common room by the student union), and she went to Harvard with her father. Lawrence is now estranged from her parents and has publicly stated that she will not repeat with her own children the hothouse teaching techniques employed by her father.

She experienced an unusual environment, but to what extent were her genes unusual too? Most of us could be in a home-school hothouse for decades without ever reaching this young girl's level of achievement or even beginning to untangle a single thread of knot theory. Did Lawrence inherit a genius gene or a whole set of mathematics-friendly genetic variations?

More worryingly, what about the other end of the spectrum: adults who never become numerically skilled enough to manage their personal finances or to carry out simple transactions without effort and distress? These people could not be further from Lawrence in their capability, but are they genetically different? Were they poorly taught? Did they miss too much school because of ill health, poor behavior, or family strife? Do they have a disability or a difficulty? If a disability, does it have specific biological markers (for example, genes) and can it be cured? If a difficulty, how can education overcome it?

Kovas's results are clear and in keeping with those found by the researchers who study reading. Her data does not support the existence of a genetically-based mathematical disability. She found that the kids doing best and worst in mathematics are just the kids who are best and worst at mathematics. They are affected by the same genes as everybody else although in varying combinations.

Like environments, genes underpin differences between people, including whether some people will be more able, healthy, or neurotic than others. Even if every child in a nation was subjected to a successful innovation in mathematics teaching, this would still be true. This is important when thinking about innovations designed to generate improvements across a whole country. Average scores will go up if the innovation is any good, but the kids at the bottom will be at least as far from the kids at the top as they were before. If the aim is to reduce the gap between the best- and worst-performing kids, then innovations need to be directed at the bottom of the distribution and not at everybody else. Extra support for the lowest achievers will also promote social mobility. The practicalities, implications, and ethics of this approach will be discussed later.

So, at a statistical level, Kovas found no genetic differences between the least able TEDS twins in mathematics and the rest of the sample, although she remains open to the possibility of rare single-gene disorders affecting mathematical ability. But what does this actually mean? If you perform a web search for "dyscalculia" you will find a wealth of information that largely converges on the view that it is "dyslexia for numbers." The British Dyslexia Association writes: "Dyscalculia is a special need and requires diagnosis and appropriate counseling as well as support away from whole class teaching." Let's think about this. The fact that those with the least ability in mathematics are not genetically distinct from everyone else is likely to come as a disappointment to some people, particularly to parents whose children struggle. But why should this be? Well, for one thing being labeled as having a medical disorder, a bona-fide learning disability, opens up more services to families and removes the stigma associated with just not being very good at something. As a society we believe that disability is more acceptable than low ability. The former implies a degree of powerlessness whereas the latter, wrongly, implies a degree of laziness or stupidity. Diagnosis brings validation. Yet the children and adults who struggle with mathematics surely have a special need either way. They have a learning difficulty, irrespective of whether that learning difficulty is classified as a medical problem. It might be that they do require support away from whole-class teaching; they almost certainly require personalized one-to-one or small-group support, either in the classroom or elsewhere. But diagnosis and counseling? For not being very good at math? Why?

Brian Butterworth, the world's leading expert on "dyscalculia," tells us that the problem affects around 6.5% of the population and describes the main difficulty for "dyscalculics" as an inability to understand what numbers mean.

> You have to help the child to understand... what "three-ness" or "four-ness" is. Such children don't have any intuition about it. They have to work it out logically. People with dyscalculia will always have trouble with math but they can compensate just as people with color-blindness learn to manage. We have to educate dyscalculic children to grasp math in a different way. (Quoted in Freeman, 2006.)

While our evidence does not support "dyscalculia" as a discrete genetic disorder, we strongly agree with Professor Butterworth's approach to children struggling with math. As he points out, you educate such children by starting from an understanding of what it is that they don't understand. You start from an individual's current level of competence and move on from there at a speed that works for that individual. In other words, you personalize their education.

The lowest-performing children in any subject have a special need (a need for extra help with that subject) but that's not the same thing as having a medical disorder. We know that mathematical ability, high or low, is influenced by genes – they are a major reason why the human species can produce both Ruth Lawrence and a kid who really doesn't get what "3" or "4" is – but Kovas's results implicate the same genes across all abilities. In other words the least able mathematicians in a class – like the least able readers – have a difficulty, not a disability. They need extra support, not a label.

Are different mathematical abilities subject to the same genetic and environmental influences?

The final question Kovas asked is whether we can think of mathematical ability as a single commodity or whether abilities in different areas of mathematics are genetically distinct. She started by exploring the links between the three areas of mathematics achievement measured by the UK national curriculum (using and applying mathematics; numbers; shapes, space and measures) and found that they were in fact very highly correlated (average correlation, 0.85). What this means in practice is that 85% of the ability that these three areas of mathematics are tapping into is common to all of them.

In a way this is not surprising: you would expect kids who are good at calculating to be good at measuring as well. It is not as if Kovas is claiming that the kids who are good at their multiplication tables are always good at basketball. Kovas also conducted a series of analyses that showed that the genes influencing one area of mathematics were largely the same as those influencing the others and that, in fact, the same genes also appear to influence other traits such as spatial abilities and language. In these analyses genes are a nameless mass. We know the same genes are involved across the different areas of mathematics assessment but not which genes in particular. This has led Kovas, with one of us (RP), to develop what has become known in the behavioral genetic literature as the "generalist genes" hypothesis. The bumper-sticker message is that genes are generalists and environments are specialists. The same genes affect a diverse range of cognitive abilities and academic achievement, but different environmental influences apply to each of these abilities. This is of vital importance for the way we educate our children. The specialist effects of the environment are precisely what a carefully calibrated classroom can offer. This is another of the founding principles upon which we will attempt our draft redesign of the school system.

In the genes ...

Kovas passed her findings to Sophia Docherty, a molecular biologist, who set to work with DNA provided by the same TEDS twins who had given us data on mathematical ability and achievement. She started where Kovas left off: 1) there is a clear genetic component to mathematical ability; 2) low mathematical ability is likely to be influenced by the same genes that affect normal variation in ability; 3) there is substantial genetic overlap between the different areas of mathematics, suggesting that genetic effects are general.

Docherty used an approach called DNA pooling, in which the DNA of large numbers of individuals is combined and subjected to a single genome-wide association scan. This is a cutting-edge method of finding genes with small effects on behavior. She found ten spots in the genome (known as single nucleotide polymorphisms or SNPs – pronounced snips) at which a letter in the genetic code commonly varied between the individuals in the sample. SNPs have two variants, so that you might inherit one DNA letter, say G, whereas a sibling inherits another, such as T; one form may confer a genetic advantage whereas the other confers a genetic risk. These ten SNPs were significantly associated with individual differences in mathematical ability and (if the research is replicated in another sample) can be said to constitute a small proportion of the genetic reasons why some people are better at mathematics than others. As expected, each individual SNP had a small effect, with the largest accounting for just over 0.5% of the differences in mathematical achievement between these 2,500 children, and the smallest only 0.13%. But when these ten DNA markers are combined to form a set they can explain 3.4% of the differences between people. This is only a first step, which requires replication, and we will need bigger and better sets of variants, but it demonstrates the direction in which genetic research is moving.

Incidentally, it is worth pointing out that when this type of research began scientists thought, or hoped, that a few genes would contribute greatly to common behaviors or disorders. In the main, this has not turned out to be the case; instead we have the QTL Hypothesis. It is, therefore, unlikely that there will ever be a time when we can make a reluctant mathematician brilliant by switching on a gene here and there.

Docherty went on to ask whether anything different was happening for the 15% of children with the lowest mathematics scores. She found that children in this group had a greater number of the less mathematics-friendly forms of the SNPs than average- and high-performing children. The one-third of TEDS children with more than half of the risk variants were almost twice as likely to be in the bottom 15% of scorers.

In other words, children at most risk will carry many of the risk variants and few positive variants, and the child with most genetic advantage will carry few risk variants and many positive variants. As the number of risk variants increases, mathematical ability will decrease. In theory this means we could test for genetic risk of low mathematical ability. But in practice these ten SNPs account for such a small amount of variance that it wouldn't tell us much even if we did. Even children in the top 15% will carry some of the risk variants and, at this stage, any cut-off would be arbitrary. And because we don't yet know the function of these genetic markers, carrying a particular version of one of them, although associated with a disadvantage in mathematics, could confer an advantage in some other area that those with the alternative version are less likely to share. After all, evolution has not seen fit to wash out these risk variants. We are beginning to map the genetics underpinnings of mathematics achievement but there is a long way yet to go.

How does Nurture Affect Mathematical Ability?

The evidence for genetic influence on individual differences in mathematical ability and achievement is conclusive, and our own research group, among others, is beginning to identify genes that may be involved. But it will take time. Surely it must be easier to identify the aspects of nurture that create differences in mathematics achievement than to identify specific genes with small individual effects? Sadly not. Research so far suggests that most aspects of the environment also have very small effects and interact with each other, and with genes, in complex ways. We can't get away with simply blaming the parents, the schools, declining standards, or food additives. The exceptions can usually be categorized as extreme-risk environments that create far more serious problems for the children who are affected by them than relatively low mathematics achievement.

In fact there have been no major genetically sensitive studies of environmental influences on mathematics achievement. Studies that analyze the influence of the home or school environment on achievement in mathematics without controlling for genetics can have value at the large scale – for example if an intervention raises average achievement across the population – but more often they just muddy the water. Consider, for example, the following three hypothetical research findings:

- Three-year-olds who spend 45 minutes a day in educational play with a parent are better at mathematics at age 10 than 3-year-olds who do not.
- Children who attend fee-paying schools have higher average mathematics scores than children who do not.
- The children of substance abusers have significantly lower average mathematics scores than other children.

It is easy to accept findings such as these at face value because very often they agree with our own prejudices and preconceptions. Of course finding time to teach children through play benefits them; of course you get a better service if you pay for it; and of course parental substance abuse has an effect on how well children thrive. But if these hypotheses are tested in a study that does not control for the effects of genes we have no real evidence that play, education, and substance abuse are genuinely environmental effects, not confounded by genes or even by other aspects of the child's environment.

Take child–parent play, for example. The parent who spends 45 minutes every day in focused, educationally relevant play with a 3-year-old child probably isn't a mother of four with a full-time job. These parents are a self-selecting sample. Not only is it possible for them to offer their child this special playtime but they are parents who have either the desire to play in this way or the belief that it will benefit their child. It is important to them that their children will go on to do well in school, and they take personal responsibility for making that happen. They also have the mental capacity and time to engage with and to stimulate their child for 45 minutes. Furthermore, they have children who, at the age of 3, can engage constructively with structured one-to-one play for 45 minutes and who enjoy mentally stimulating, educational play, perhaps because they are just naturally good at it.

So, if researchers find that early one-to-one play of this nature is associated with mathematics achievement at school, then this relationship may exist for any number of reasons. Maybe children who are naturally good at mathematics or related skills such as puzzles and problem-solving evoke that kind of play from their parents whereas other children with different appetites and aptitudes invite different kinds of play such as role play, messy play, or physical play – what we would call an evocative genotype–environment correlation. Maybe the parents who focus on their children in this way at age 3 are similarly hands-on throughout school, making sure they help their child or find help for them whenever they show signs of not having understood something. Maybe both the parents and the children involved are naturally conscientious; always keen to do the right thing whatever they happen to want to do. The cliché used in first-year undergraduate psychology courses is that although umbrella use is correlated with rainfall, putting up umbrellas does not actually cause the rain to fall. In other words, correlation does not imply causation.

The same applies to the fee-paying schools and substance-abuse examples. Attendance at a fee-paying school may correlate with mathematics achievement because the parents who can afford the fees are academic achievers themselves and have passed on the ability to jump through academic hoops to their children through a biological rather than a social mechanism. These children may need relatively little input to succeed, so their higher scores in mathematics may have nothing whatsoever to do with the quality of education offered in the school. They are naturally bright kids who would perform well anywhere. The children with substance-abusing parents may inherit risk-taking personality traits that make sitting quietly and learning mathematics skills unappealing to them. They may fail for both genetic and environmental reasons. By failing to control for the effects of genes, most studies leave us none the wiser.

So, if we're serious about figuring out how to raise mathematics achievement – and we should be – we need to begin by taking genes into account and by deciding whose mathematics achievement we want to raise. Is it the national average that needs a boost, or just the low achievers, or the underachievers, the girls, the boys, or the kids who want to work with numbers? We need to generate hypotheses by looking at the influences that appear to be effective, and we need to statistically control for genetic effects until we reach the stage where we know what goes on at the biological level. And, most important of all, we need to explore the influence that genes and environments have on each other so that we can understand which environments will be most beneficial to which children. Only by engaging with genetics can we truly find a way to teach mathematics more effectively to every child.

References

Freeman, H. (2006). Inside story: dyscalculia. *The Times*, 10 June 2006.

Gladwell, M. (2008). *Outliers: The Story of Success*. New York: Little, Brown and Company.

Schilpp, P.A. (Ed.) (1949). *Albert Einstein, Philosopher-Scientist*. Evanston, IL: Open Court.

Further Reading

Docherty, S.J., Davis, O.S.P., Kovas, Y., Meaburn, E.L., Dale, P.S., Petrill, S.A., Schalkwyk L.C., and Plomin, R. (2010). A genome-wide association study identifies multiple loci associated with mathematics ability and disability. *Genes, Brain and Behavior*, 9, 234–247. This first GWAS study of math finds the usual result of many genes of small effect.

Kovas, Y., Haworth, C.M.A., Dale, P.S., and Plomin, R. (2007). *The Genetic and Environmental Origins of Learning Abilities and Disabilities in the Early School Years*. Monographs of the Society for Research in Child Development 72 (3). New York, Oxford: Wiley-Blackwell. A detailed account of TEDS findings related to school achievement and cognitive ability in the elementary school years.

Kovas, Y., Doherty, S., Davis, O., Meaburn , E., Dale, P.S., Petrill, Schalkwyk, L., and Plomin, R. (2009). Generalist genes and mathematics: The latest quantitative and molecular genetic results from the TEDS study. *Behavior Genetics*, 39(6), 663–664. More detail on the generalist genes hypothesis. What matters most for schools is the finding that environments are specialists.

Chapter 5

Physical Education: Who, What, Why, Where, and How?

In November 2011, sports and exercise medicine expert Dr Andrew Franklyn-Miller issued a statement to the effect that the build-up to the London 2012 Olympic Games represented the perfect chance to encourage British children to become more active. He argued that the Olympics could give the United Kingdom a unique opportunity to promote healthy and active lifestyles, but that the opportunity was being missed. The fact that one in three British 10- and 11-year-olds was classed as overweight or obese was, argued Franklyn-Miller, indefensible: "We have our children in one place for seven hours a day. Maybe we should start influencing their physical literacy, their health, and their wellbeing, when we've got them in front of us." In this chapter we explore what genetic research can tell us about whether there is a role for education in improving the health of a nation, and how that might work.

School, according to Franklyn-Miller, is the place to turn things around, and he suggested doing so by making physical literacy the subject of compulsory testing in the same way as mathematics,

G is for Genes: The Impact of Genetics on Education and Achievement, First Edition.
Kathryn Asbury and Robert Plomin.
© 2014 John Wiley & Sons, Inc. Published 2014 by John Wiley & Sons, Inc.

reading, and writing. A backlash against the idea of more testing followed immediately, but Franklyn-Miller believes that without mandatory testing – and clearly defined steps to help children who fall short – nothing will change. But are school sports really the solution to the problem? And is school the appropriate place to tackle medical, rather than purely academic, issues? Let's re-examine Franklyn-Miller's ideas in the light of our understanding of how genes and environments work.

There are several questions to ask about whether and how schools can influence sporting prowess and health outcomes, given the role of genes – and whether it is appropriate for them to do so. For instance, does genetic influence on fitness, obesity, and heart disease render school hours spent on PE – let alone the extra layer of complication that a formal and formally assessed physical literacy curriculum would entail – redundant? And, if environment influences any or all of these health outcomes then is it shared or nonshared environmental influence that matters more? For example, if fitness or fatness show a lot of shared environmental influence but very little nonshared environmental influence, then Dr Franklyn-Miller's suggestion, which involves planned fitness routines and testing of "a PE curriculum that embraces push, pull, squat, brace, rotate, accelerate, and change of direction" might just work. If, however, nonshared environment is the driver then a one-size-fits-all approach will not achieve what it sets out to achieve.

The best studies of physical activity in the school years have tended to be carried out on teenagers, and we know from them that regular moderate exercise decreases and sedentary behavior increases between the ages of 13 and 19. Because of known links between a sedentary lifestyle and later health problems this is a matter of concern for policy makers in education, health, and health economics. There are several possible causes of this phenomenon. For instance, at 13 PE is still compulsory in schools, and parents are likely to organize their children and ferry them to training, matches, and competitions. By 19 most sport that takes place happens out of school and is organized by the young people themselves, requiring more motivation and love of the activities in question. Also, during this time both academic and social pressures increase, and although keeping active may be seen as a priority at the younger ages it begins to play second fiddle to getting good grades and fitting in with friends. The physical changes and social embarrassments associated with puberty may also increase reluctance to get into sports kit and run around. Notes from home excusing pupils from PE certainly seem to become more commonplace in high school.

Just as the prevalence of exercise changes over the teenage years so, too, does the pattern of heritability. The relationship between genes and exercise for young children is a new but blossoming area of research, fueled by the fact that in many developed nations the age of onset of obesity is falling. One UK study run by obesity researchers and behavioral geneticists looked at the heritability of physical activity in 9- and 11-year-olds and found that shared environment was by far the strongest influence on physical activity for boys and girls (Fisher *et al.*, 2010). At these ages it appears that schools and families are well placed to encourage physical activity, and that Dr Franklyn-Miller's proposal, or something like it, might well make a difference in primary schools and in the early years of secondary school.

A study of Dutch twins, however, looked at activity levels between the ages of 13 and 19 and saw that the influence of the shared environment waned to almost nothing by age 15 (van der Aa *et al.*, 2010). Similar results have been found in Belgian and Portuguese studies (e.g., Maia, Thomis, and Beunen, 2002). In the early to mid teens, genes and nonshared experiences became more powerful drivers of exercise frequency, duration, and intensity, with genes explaining more than 75% of the differences in physical activity. Nonshared experiences might include being picked for a school team, winning or losing a race, being picked last in class, being bullied or praised because of sporting prowess, or being exposed to a form of exercise that suits an individual child. And of course children may be genetically predisposed to seeking out, finding, or evoking experiences such as these. Shared environmental experiences had virtually no influence on these teenagers.

The researchers in the Dutch study hypothesized that the strong genetic effects we see on physical activity levels by adolescence may actually reflect strong genetic effects on sporting ability. In this case what we see is an active genotype–environment correlation in which young people who have a talent for physical activity continue to engage in it whereas those who are not genetically predisposed to enjoy and be good at sports drop out as soon as they are allowed to. However, exercise is good for us whether we enjoy it or not and a sedentary life takes its toll, so it seems unreasonable simply to go with the flow. What is less clear is whether it is the responsibility of schools to address what is, after all, primarily a public health issue.

As we have already made clear, our view is that education today has two primary purposes. The first is to get all children to a good level of skill in literacy, numeracy, and ICT. The second is to provide them with opportunities to identify and develop their talents and special abilities, their own unique selling points when they come to negotiate their niche in the world. Offering a wide range of physical activities to pupils seems to be an important and necessary aspect of this second aim of education. Therefore, the option to choose sporting activities should be available, as it already is to a greater or lesser extent, at every age and in every school. But should sport and exercise be compulsory and, if so, for how long?

The health of the nation does not figure in the hierarchy of educational priorities we have proposed. Franklyn-Miller is undeniably right that school is the umbrella under which the largest possible number of young people can be gathered, and it does afford us an opportunity to influence their future. But are schools responsible for all aspects of a child's future? Should they be teaching them to cook, clean, drive, form and maintain successful relationships, bring up children, manage their money, and sell stuff on eBay? Maybe, but this is a political and social question rather than a scientific one . . . and there are only so many hours in the school day.

What empirical genetic research can offer to the debate is some evidence about which approaches might work and which are likely to be wasted, whatever underlying political philosophy prevails at the time. In this respect the evidence suggests that there would be health benefits from compulsory PE throughout school, and even beyond the years of compulsory education for those who stay on. A unified PE curriculum seems likely to encourage fitness and activity but only until the early secondary school years. With this in mind it seems wise to offer a wide range of choices even to young children, and to allow some degree of specialization, because by 14 or 15 at the latest pupils will only exercise if they enjoy the particular method involved. It makes sense, therefore, to find out what they can do and what they enjoy doing before secondary school (middle school in the United States) and invest in it early. After the first year or so of secondary school the curriculum should be entirely choice-driven. The girl who hates netball might love yoga or golf; the boy who hates hockey might have a talent for ballroom dancing or climbing. Primary school is the place for a two-pronged attack, promoting fitness through a unified PE curriculum and promoting a taste for exercise through individualization and choice. Finding a form of exercise that each child likes could set them up to make healthy choices in adolescence and perhaps for the rest of their lives.

If children find ways that are acceptable to them of maintaining fit bodies and a healthy lifestyle then the benefits to society and to the economy could be vast, not to mention to the individuals themselves. Given that sport will not be the personal choice or talent of every child, this is the best argument for keeping up PE throughout school. On balance we think, like Dr Franklyn-Miller, that using education to make children healthier is a goal with considerable social merit. But how achievable is such a goal? What impact can school-based PE lessons hope to have on complex social issues such as smoking, obesity, and overall fitness? Again, genetic research can give us some clues.

Genes, Sports, and Smoking

Smoking bans have been enforced in public spaces in countries around the world. Cigarettes, in packets with warnings that SMOKING KILLS, are also increasingly expensive, and yet teenagers continue to be drawn to the habit, or at least to an initial drag with friends. Peer pressure plays a part, as does the desire to appear grown-up or cool. But behind these commonplace explanations there is an interesting story involving both genes and PE.

A study conducted by a team at the University of Pennsylvania sheds new light on the relationship between sports, and smoking. The researchers set out to explore reasons why some adolescents progress from a trial puff at a cigarette to a regular smoking habit while others do not (Audrain-McGovern *et al.*, 2006). There were certain patterns that had already been identified from previous smoking research. For instance, almost 25% of adolescents are regular smokers, and the prevalence of smoking increases throughout adolescence. Physical activity and team sport participation are known to decrease over that same time frame. Furthermore, physically active teenagers are about half as likely to smoke as others, and young people who become less involved in team sports as they progress through school are almost three times more likely to become regular smokers than those who maintain their involvement. Even without emerging evidence from genetics these statistics represent a strong argument for encouraging physical activity and team sport participation from a young age and, crucially, doing what you can to help teenagers to maintain their involvement even as pressures and temptations – exams and social life as well as cigarettes – grow. The researchers reasoned, on the basis of these figures, that perhaps physical activity protects teenagers from being attracted to and then addicted to cigarettes in a tangible way.

But of course this is not a simple story with a simple solution. If it were then smoking would have gone the same way as snuff-taking by now, and teenagers everywhere would be leaping out of bed on a Saturday morning to get to their volleyball league game. While there is a relationship between physical activity and teenage smoking we also know that individual differences in smoking are influenced by genes, and we even have a couple of candidate genes. A dopamine reuptake transporter called SLC6A3 and the dopamine D_2 receptor DRD2 have been found to be smoking risk genotypes, and teenagers who carry the risky versions of one or both of these genes appear, on the basis of this research, to be more likely to become regular smokers. In fact, their chance of progressing to regular smoking appears to double with each DRD2-A1 allele they carry. Both of these genes affect the dopamine pathway, and the risky versions of both are carried by almost 20% of teenagers. More than 30% carry at least one of them, potentially putting a significant minority of young people at genetic risk for developing a potentially deadly and certainly expensive smoking habit. As with all such candidate gene studies replication is a priority, but this research does suggest that genetic influence is relevant to debates about smoking prevention.

One of the functions of dopamine is as a mechanism by which we perceive reward. The Pennsylvania researchers hypothesized that teenagers who carry the A1 allele of the DRD2 gene (or the 10 repeat allele of the SLC6A3 gene) have low dopamine activity and, since nicotine boosts dopamine activity, smoking may be more rewarding to them. In other words, nicotine is likely to give more of a buzz to these teenagers than to those who do not carry the risky variants of the genes.

However, as usual, genes are not deterministic and nicotine is not the only way to boost dopamine concentrations. There's almost always more than one way to skin a cat. Research with animals (not cat-skinning we hasten to add) has shown that exercise has a very similar effect to nicotine on dopamine concentrations and therefore represents an alternative and safer way of gaining the same chemical reward. In other words, the buzz that kids at genetic risk of developing a regular smoking habit get from tobacco might reasonably be replaced by sport. To put numbers on it, physical activity was associated with 37% of the differences between the teenagers in the study in terms of their smoking progression, although this could represent either cause or effect.

Another possible explanation is that team sports affect the genetic propensity to smoke through social mechanisms such as anti-smoking messages from coaches and team-mates. This social mechanism may reinforce the chemical message of the dopamine boost induced by sport. This is a nice example of a gene–environment interaction where the effect of genes, in this case a negative effect, is turned on its head by environmental means. The genetically programmed dopamine boost is replaced by an environmental one.

In summary, the researchers found that being involved in team sports protected teenagers from becoming regular smokers, even if they carried genes that predisposed them to picking up or maintaining the habit, and that the protective effects could partly be explained by the physical activity involved. So what does this mean for school sports? Well, at the simplest level it seems that efforts to prevent adolescent smoking should focus on helping teenagers to identify at least one sport in which they are prepared to participate. On the basis of this research, assuming you accept a disease prevention role for school sports, then identifying sports (perhaps especially team sports) to suit individual children appears to be a valid and worthwhile goal for secondary school PE. It is for society to decide whether this is a good use of school time.

Obesity, Genes, and Environment

The second issue we address in this chapter is obesity. Can school sports realistically tackle the worsening obesity problem in the developed world? (Kelly *et al.*, 2008) In theory it should be possible, as obesity is correlated with a sedentary lifestyle. However, other environmental influences are also linked to obesity, such as low socioeconomic status, stress, and low levels of education. Not to mention food. For the first time in history, in the developed world, the poor are more likely than the rich to carry too much fat. Furthermore, environmental triggers must lie behind the recent obesity epidemic because the gene pool could not possibly have changed quickly enough to account for it.

However, and this sounds like a contradiction, genes are the strongest influence on both Body Mass Index (BMI) and obesity (Grilo and Pogue-Geile, 1991; Dubois *et al.*, 2012). It is important to remember that height is genetic too, one of the most genetic of human traits in fact, and yet people continue to get taller because of improving health and nutrition. BMI is almost as genetic as height, and genes affect differences between us in terms of weight, but experience can still make changes across the board. It is likely that obesity is increasing at the population level for environmental reasons – for instance, the availability and low cost of certain types of food, and a reduction in physical activity (Skelton *et al.*, 2011). Genes cannot cause an average population increase in obesity but they do influence the differences between us (Wardle *et al.*, 2008). Research carried out with the TEDS twins at ages 7 and 10 concluded that genes could account for 60% of the differences between children in terms of their body fat at age 7 and 74% at age 10. In spite of the twins in our study living in the same home and attending the same school the influence of shared environment is low and gets lower as the children get older. So we can't just blame Mum for being over-enthusiastic with the fried food. Shared environmental influence accounts for 40% of the body fat differences between children at birth, 22% at age 7, and only 12% by age 10. This suggests, for example, that one-size-fits-all interventions such as Franklyn-Miller's are probably not the best way to go in tackling obesity. A series of health education or exercise classes held in all schools could possibly reduce the average weight, but obese children will remain obese or at least overweight. Trying to leverage genotype–environment correlations by targeting obese children, or those at risk of becoming so, using nonshared environmental interventions is a more complex but almost certainly more fruitful way to go.

Because of the strong genetic influence involved, weight control is likely to be more difficult for children with a greater than average complement of "weight gain" genes. In time, DNA testing will allow us to identify these children at a young age and provide early support. This early prediction is likely to lead to prevention methods that are far more powerful than our current attempts to "fix" the problem. Meanwhile, physical activity-based interventions tailored to individual children are likely to be one good approach to tackling obesity and its long-term health consequences. This means identifying the activities individual children are most likely to enjoy and participate in willingly. However, it takes a lot of exercise to burn your cookie calories, and exercise is likely to be just one part of a broader prevention strategy. There seems to be a role for the schools to act as one of several possible referring bodies to clinics and health settings. On balance, we think that tackling the obesity problem is not the job of school sports.

With obesity, food as well as exercise is an obvious consideration. Although parents feed their children wildly different diets at home, all children eat in school once a day. In some cases they eat a hot meal prepared at or for the school and in some cases they bring in a packed lunch from home. In some countries, including the United Kingdom, children from the poorest families are entitled to a free hot school meal. In recent years the United Kingdom has debated school dinners in an unprecedentedly public and heated way. Celebrity chef Jamie Oliver spearheaded a campaign for healthy school meals, gaining the ear of the government and the opprobrium of disgruntled parents. One of these, dubbed "the meat pie Mum," famously pushed cheeseburgers through the school railings to her children to counteract the perilous effects of vegetables newly on offer in the school canteen. It made for good TV and journalistic high jinks, but the campaign has been criticized for forcing change too quickly and reducing the uptake of school dinners in favor of packed lunches.

Children's diets will vary enormously, and when most food is consumed at home there is only so much that schools can do to tackle obesity on this front. Food is largely a private rather than a public matter. Even universal cookery classes are probably not the answer for the majority, because shared environmental influence disappears at the age at which they might provide lasting benefits. This means that, because shared environment does not show much influence on obesity, an identical and compulsory healthy lunch in every school in the country would not make a marked difference to obesity rates. However, in support of a PE curriculum designed to foster healthy choices it makes sense that lunches cooked in school are nutritionally balanced and that there should be restrictions as to what can and cannot be included in packed lunches.

In summary, weight has been found to be highly susceptible to genetic influence but the environment also has an important role to play. The research carried out so far suggests that the average weight of a nation of school children could be moderately affected by positive shared environmental influences in the early school years, although probably not by the secondary school years. Both the problem and the evidence suggest that it would be better to focus time and resources on overweight and obese children and to individualize their weight-loss programs by focusing on exercise they enjoy and other healthy living strategies that work for them as individuals. While some of this can be tackled in school PE sessions, by offering a wide enough range of exercise opportunities to attract everyone, it is likely that the affected children will need separate individualized support in a health rather than a school setting.

The Heritability of Fitness

Obesity and smoking both have a negative impact on fitness. Usain Bolt does not nourish his lightning-fast body with Mars Bars and Marlboros. However, fitness is affected by more than food and exercise. Professor Claude Bouchard and colleagues on the HER-ITAGE Family Study have looked at variation in fitness among research participants with sedentary lifestyles. He arranged for one group of Canadians to be trained in exactly the same manner as each other for around five months and then examined changes in their fitness over that time. Bouchard found that people responded to their identical training in very different ways. Using VO_{2max}

(maximal aerobic capacity) as his index of fitness he found that although the average gain was 33% as a result of the training program, one individual gained 88% while another increased by only 5%. Professor Bouchard also used average power output sustained on a bicycle for 90 minutes as a measure of actual performance and again saw substantial variation in spite of the fact that all participants had experienced the same training program. Overall, performance soared by an average of 51% after 20 weeks. Everyone improved as a result of the training. However, the biggest gainer's actual performance far exceeded that of the smallest gainer. Bouchard proposed that there are "responders" and "non-responders." He also suggested that, because the timescale of training responsiveness varied between people, there was a category of "late bloomers." While some improved a great deal within the first six weeks they then reached a plateau, whereas others were stagnant for the first six to ten weeks before the benefits of training really began to show. The same nurture does not benefit everyone in the same way, further reinforcing our argument that the type of athletic ability kids and adults are capable of varies enormously and needs to be drawn out in different, personalized ways.

Bouchard's team explored this phenomenon further using a genetically sensitive research design. They ran another 20-week training program, but this time for ten pairs of identical twins. The twins trained for 45-minute sessions four to five times each week with average training intensity set close to 80% of maximal heart rate. By the end of the program average aerobic power had increased by 14% (these participants were not chosen for being sedentary at the start so the increase was not as striking) and ventilatory threshold (the exercise intensity at which breathing rate begins to increase dramatically) by 17%. Increase in VO_{2max} was pretty much the same for both twins in a pair but it differed between pairs of twins, suggesting that training interacts with different genomes to different effect. We know that genes make a difference to response to training here because MZ twins responded in virtually the same way as each other (See Bouchard *et al.*, 1999). As part of his HERITAGE Family Study Professor Bouchard and his colleagues have more recently begun to identify some of the genes associated with the "trainability" of VO_{2max} such as the muscle form of the creatine kinase gene CKM. This is significant research with important health implications because regular endurance exercise has been shown to have a positive impact on our risk of both cardiovascular disease and Type 2 diabetes.

So what does this imply for physical education in schools and extracurricular sports clubs? If some kids are unlikely to benefit much is it a waste of time for them? The way to answer these questions definitively is to carry out a large-scale twin study of activity levels and response to PE interventions and see what happens. In the meantime we have to go with what we know, which is that sporting ability and fitness are heritable but not genetically determined. Also, we know that shared influences such as school sports have a big impact at least until the teenage years. Using this information to trigger positive choices, positive genotype–environment correlations, is the best way forward. Primary education, therefore, represents an opportunity to improve general fitness but also to provide choices that will allow children to find and nurture a real talent or at least a way of exercising that they enjoy, or can put up with.

Gym Class Heroes

So far we have looked at whether, from a genetic point of view, it is worth teaching PE in school at all and what benefits might accrue for children in general. But what about the kids with a real talent for sport, the ones who could become world class and compete at the highest level? What underlies their success and what can schools do to nurture them and support them in developing their full potential?

> These are my new shoes. They're good shoes. They won't make you rich like me, they won't make you rebound like me, they definitely won't make you handsome like me. They'll only make you have shoes like me. That's it.
>
> (Charles Barkley, commercial for basketball shoes.)

For style-conscious hero-worshipping teenagers the shoes might be enough. But what about the others, the ones who want the looks, the money, and, most especially, the rebound? Swedish exercise physiologist Per-Olof Astrand once said that the best thing an aspiring athlete can do is choose the right parents. His implication is clear; sports stars are born not made. Another school of thought claims that elite standards in sport are the result of extensive and expert training. The two camps (innate versus training) mirror the old nature versus nurture debate. If there is anything we can predict with complete confidence it is that athletic performance, even at the very top end of ability, will involve both genes and experience... because human endeavor invariably does.

Much more research needs to be carried out in this field if we are to explore the relative and interdependent roles of genes and experience. However, this hasn't stopped a handful of companies in the United States and Australia from peddling DNA tests to pushy parents who want to know how likely their toddlers are to be successful in sport, and to identify sports in which to encourage them. Dr Theodore Friemann, Director of San Diego's Medical Center's Interdepartmental Gene Therapy program has branded this "an opportunity to sell new versions of snake oil."

In fact, the claim is based on good research. As is often the case in science, it is the application that is misleading. Professor Kathryn North works on the genetics of rare neuromuscular diseases at the University of Sydney. In the course of her research she began to focus on a gene called ACTN3, which controls the production of protein in muscles, making it a good bet for a neuromuscular diseases researcher. Professor North found that the patients she studied were deficient in the protein alpha-actinin-3, which is produced by ACTN3. However, she also found that healthy relatives of the patients lacked this protein too, as did several members of the research team. The team went on to discover that almost one-fifth of white Caucasians share this deficiency, although most do not succumb to neuromuscular diseases (Yang *et al.*, 2003). They pursued the link further.

Alpha-actinin-3 is found in fast-twitch muscles, the type that are used to make powerful movements such as sprinting and jumping. One could reasonably predict that the likes of Usain Bolt, for example, have a very healthy dose of this protein. Everybody inherits two copies of ACTN3, one from their mother and one from their father. The two key variants of the gene are known as R and X. The X allele stops muscle cells from reading the entire code of ACTN3 and if you inherit two copies of the X version you will be unable to produce any alpha-actinin-3 at all. Professor North and her researchers reasoned that if there is a variation in the human population, people who have two R versions of ACTN3 might be better at sprinting and power sports than those with only one R or, worse still, two Xs.

In conjunction with the Australian Institute of Sport the team took DNA from more than 4,000 elite athletes from a wide range of sports and compared it with that of a control sample. They found that power and sprint athletes did in fact tend to have two working versions of the ACTN3 gene (RR) but, perhaps more surprisingly, they also found that endurance athletes had two deficient versions (XX). In other words, they found that what was originally perceived as a deficiency (the X version) actually benefited slow, efficient muscle performance. "When the Lord closes a door," as the Abbess in *The Sound of Music* puts it, "somewhere He opens a window." It was on the back of this research that ACTN3 became dubbed "the speed gene" and companies like Genetics Technologies in Victoria, Australia, and Atlas Sports Genetics in Boulder, Colorado, began to sell the DNA testing kits especially targeting 2- to 8-year-olds.

The idea is that children under the age of 8 are too young to show their natural aptitude through their performance alone. Therefore, another method is needed if appropriate training is to start young and time is not to be wasted on finger painting or playing tag when it could be spent on kick-starting potentially profitable or glorious sporting careers. Those marketing the tests claim that kids with the RR version of the gene should be encouraged in power sports such as sprinting and jumping whereas those with the XX version of the gene should be encouraged in endurance sports like, erm . . . , marathon running, or rowing? (It is rather difficult to think of appropriate endurance sports for the under-8s.) Those with the more common XR version of ACTN3 get to choose for themselves, but we are not told the odds of them excelling in either. Are they doubly enabled? Are they doomed to mediocrity? Or should they focus on sports that require both speed and endurance, maybe martial arts? The whole enterprise suggests that a DNA test can tell you whether you should enter your child in the obstacle course or the egg and spoon race at preschool sports day. It suggests that pigeonholing children by using DNA tests to override their developing interests, preferences, and aptitudes is a good idea, and furthermore that tailored training is a good thing for a young child's developing body. It suggests, to be perfectly honest, that pushy parents too often have more money than sense and that wily, clued-up entrepreneurs know exactly how to exploit this.

Let's be clear. Two X versions of ACTN3 might make a minuscule contribution to Usain Bolt's competitive edge, and at the very highest levels of sport a minuscule advantage can make the difference between winning gold or silver, or making or missing the national squad. Two R versions might have been a boost to Haile Gebrselassie and Steve Redgrave in their sporting careers for similar reasons, but for your child – particularly at this early stage in their development – this gene is just one small cherry in a big cherry pie. Many other genes influence athletic prowess, body size and shape, fitness, response to training, and willingness to train in the first place. And that's before we get started on environmental influences. Maybe training too hard too young will have a negative influence on athletic potential? We would propose that the desperation for success shown by the parents who buy these tests is likely to be a much stronger influence on their children's development, and their relationship with sport, than alpha-actinin-3 levels or allelic variation in the ACTN3 gene. See what your children enjoy, what they gravitate towards, and support them in their choices. And if they're not ready to make choices at age 2, 4, 6 or 8, don't worry about it. A DNA test can tell you with devastating certainty if your child is suffering from a rare single-gene disorder, in which case choosing a sporting activity will not be your top priority, but as yet it cannot predict your child's talents or their developmental trajectory. It is our belief that in time we will know much more about which genes are linked with which behaviors, and that this will help us to tailor opportunities to children, but that a DNA test will never be able to predict the future with certainty because genes do not work alone.

It is also impossible to think of a sport simple enough to require a single action that could be determined by a single gene. For example, swimmers need to control their arms, hands, fingers, legs, feet, toes, lungs, and heads, and combine them in motions that have grace and efficiency as well as speed and power. They also have to maintain the motivation to train regularly and, when in a race, they need the drive to fend off the competition and win. To do this they need mental strength to battle nerves, to compete against their peers, and to combine every requirement of their sport to the very best of their ability. The requirements are different for each sport and, in particular, there are differences between individual-performance sports such as gymnastics, sports that resemble one-on-one combat, such as tennis, and team sports such as football. Some sports are more dependent on power, mental strength, strategy, or speed than others, but all require a range of skills and therefore all are highly complex behaviors depending on a whole multitude of genes and experiences, thereby sitting comfortably within the framework of the QTL hypothesis.

We know about many genes that could be linked to athletic performance. We know that many anatomical and physical attributes are heavily influenced by genes, much more so than complex behaviors, and that some of these are important markers for sporting success. For example, the heart's coronary network – the distribution and size of blood vessels within your heart – is highly heritable. So too is the branching pattern of blood vessels leading to the lungs; total heart size; muscle proteins; muscle fiber composition; and metabolism of fat. All of these attributes are relevant to fitness and athletic performance, making it clear that your parents and ancestors do make a difference to your aptitude for sporting success. Interestingly, if you fancy becoming an endurance athlete, the genes you inherit from your mother and her ancestral line are more important in one sense than those you inherit from your father. This is because much of the energy required for endurance sports is stored in mitochondria, tiny structures inside muscle cells. Mitochondria have their own genes, and all of the mitochondria in your body come from your mother, because eggs contain mitochondria while sperm do not.

So genes matter, but they don't determine anything. Your genetic inheritance works in conjunction with your training, nutrition, motivation, other preferences – you may have a taste for playing long, demanding piano concertos rather than running long, demanding races – and chance experiences. It does not operate in a vacuum. Genes do, however, have significant predictive power and, understood well and used wisely, can underpin the choices we make for ourselves and our children. As with the 3Rs, if everyone on the planet was given the same sporting education and opportunities there would be almost as much variability in athletic performance as there is now, although average performance would improve. With the best nurture in the world not all of us can make it to the top in every, or even one, sport. But without the best nurture, future Olympians, world champions, and world-class team players will fall by the wayside. Nature requires nurture, and different natures require different nurture.

In Summary . . .

So, in the light of genetic research, what does sport, and particularly school sport, mean for the majority of young people who fall short of being world-class? Well, like most school subjects, one would hope to make it enjoyable for pupils but, as with mathematics, literature, and science, that is not an educational end in itself. PE can be used to foster personal attributes such as motivation, competitiveness, teamwork, and confidence; however, whether these alone are acceptable educational goals is also open to discussion. The decision on whether or not the subject should be taught at all is really one for politicians and society at large to decide.

If PE is to be taught, then genetically sensitive research suggests that a standardized program could have a beneficial influence on younger children, but that older children need to be offered more choices if they are to continue to feel the same benefits. The key is to use the primary school years, before genes take the wheel, to promote a taste for exercise and to introduce children to a wide range of exercise options. That way they can make informed decisions about how they want to pursue PE when they reach secondary school. The emerging evidence that sports participation for teenagers may be related to smoking is also interesting and suggests that including a compulsory exercise module even in choice-driven curricula for 16–18-year-olds might yield benefits.

In this chapter we have described research showing that both the amount and the quality of physical activity we engage in is influenced by genes, and that genetic influence gets stronger the further behind we leave childhood. We also looked at genetic influences on smoking, obesity, fitness, and elite athletic performance. We saw that shared environmental influence does have a strong impact on physical activity levels in young children but that the effect tails away during the first few years of high school. Beyond that, genes and nonshared experiences are the key influences and, at this stage, environmental interventions have to be of the nonshared kind – personalized – if they are to have any effect at all on young people's activity levels. In Part Two of this book, we'll put all of this genetic theory into practice and attempt to answer the who, what, why, where, and how of Physical Education.

References

Audrain-McGovern, J., Rodriguez, D., Wileyto, P., Schmitz, K.H., and Shields, P.G. (2006). Effect of team sport participation on genetic predisposition to adolescent smoking progression. *Archives of General Psychiatry*, 63 (4), 433–441.

Bouchard, C., An, P., Rice, T., Skinner, J. S., Wilmore, J. H., Gagnon, J., and Rao, D. C. (1999). Familial aggregation of VO_{2max} response to exercise training: results from the HERITAGE Family Study. *Journal of Applied Physiology*, 87(3), 1003–1008.

Dubois, L., Ohm Kyvik, K., Girard, M., Tatone-Takuda, F., Perusse, D., Hjelmborg, J., Wright, M.J., Lichtenstein, P., and Martin, N.G. (2012). Genetic and environmental contributions to weight, height, and BMI from birth to 19 years of age: An international study of over 12,000 twin pairs. *PLoS One*, 7:e30153.

Fisher, A., van Jaarsveld, C.H.M., Llewellyn, C.H., and Wardle, J. (2010). Environmental influences on children's physical activity: Quantitative estimates using a twin design. *PLoS ONE* 5 (4): e10110.

Grilo, C.M. and Pogue-Geile, M.F. (1991). The nature of environmental influences on weight and obesity: A behaviour genetic analysis. *Psychological Bulletin*, 10, 520–537.

Kelly, T., Yang, W., Chen, C.S., Reynolds, K., and He, J. (2008). Global burden of obesity in 2005 and projections to 2030. *International Journal of Obesity*, 32, 1431–1437.

Franklyn-Miller, A. (2011). Missed Olympic opportunity to get children exercising. *BBC News*, 21 November.

Maia, J.A.R., Thomis, M., and Beunen, G. (2002). Genetic Factors in physical activity levels: a twin study. *American Journal of Preventive Medicine*, 23 (2) (Supp 1) 87–91.

Skelton, J.A., Irby, M.B., Grzywacz, J.G., and Miller, G. (2011). Etiologies of obesity in children: Nature and nurture. *Pediatric Clinics of North America*, 58, 1333–1354.

Van der Aa, N., De Geus, E.J.C., van Beijsterveldt, T.C.E.M., Boomsma, D.I., and Bartels, M. (2010). Genetic influences on individual differences in exercise behavior during adolescence. *International Journal of Pediatrics*, 138345.

Wardle, J., Carnell, S., Haworth, C.M.A., and Plomin, R. (2008). Evidence for a strong genetic influence on childhood adiposity despite the force of the obesogenic environment. *American Journal of Clinical Nutrition*, 87, 398–404.

Yang, N., MacArthur, D. G., Gulbin, J. P., Hahn, A. G., Beggs, A. H., Easteal, S., and North, K. (2003). ACTN3 genotype is associated with human elite athletic performance. *The American Journal of Human Genetics*, 73(3), 627–631.

Further Reading

For further information on Professor Claude Bouchard's ongoing work on genetic and environmental influences on fitness and fatness and the HERITAGE Family Study, go to: www.pbrc.edu/heritage (accessed 17 June 2013).

For a detailed review of genetically sensitive research into smoking behavior try: Rose, R.J., Broms, U., Korhonen, T., Dick, D.M., and Kaprio, J. (2009). Genetics of smoking behavior. In Y.-K. Kim (ed.) *Handbook of Behavior Genetics* (pp. 411–432). New York: Springer.

Smoking research becomes ever more nuanced. This paper, for instance, presents evidence that how people experience their first ever cigarettes is influenced by genes and nonshared environmental influence. Haberstick, B.C., Ehringer, M.A., Lessem, J.M., Hopfer, C.J., and Hewitt, J.K. (2011). Dizziness and the genetic influences on subjective experiences of initial cigarette use. *Addiction*, 106, 391–399.

Chapter 6

Science: A Different Way of Thinking?

It is difficult to read the lists of Nobel Prize-winning scientists and not to notice that they are mostly men. Only about 2% of Nobel Prizes for science have been awarded to women. Why should this be? Are men wired to be better scientists? Does society provide an environment that is more conducive to scientific achievement for boys and men than for girls and women? Both theories are proposed with great regularity.

Furthermore, the Nobel Prize for science lists, as well as being male-dominated, are littered with family relationships. There's Niels Bohr and his son Aage, father and son physicists William Henry Bragg and William Lawrence Bragg, Manne and Kai Siegbahn, Hans von Euler-Chelpin and his son Ulf von Euler, C.V. Raman and his nephew Subrahmanyan Chandrasekhar, and Arthur and Roger Kornberg. There are even women represented among the Nobel Laureate families, notably Marie Curie, her husband Pierre and their daughter, Irene Joliot-Curie. What set them all off on the path to Stockholm? What combination of genes and

G is for Genes: The Impact of Genetics on Education and Achievement, First Edition.
Kathryn Asbury and Robert Plomin.
© 2014 John Wiley & Sons, Inc. Published 2014 by John Wiley & Sons, Inc.

environment – and the interplay between them – lies behind these striking family resemblances? If you did well in physics, chemistry, or biology at school, what are the odds that your sons will do well too? And your daughters? If you did badly, what are the odds that your children are doomed, regardless of their sex? What difference will it make if they are your adopted children rather than your biological children? Can your expertise make a major difference to children who do not share your genes?

Genetic research can shed some light on these debates. Dr Claire Haworth has used data gathered from TEDS twins to explore genetic and environmental influences on achievement in science, and differences between boys and girls. She began her research by asking whether science would behave in the same way as literacy and mathematics in terms of its genetic and environmental etiology. We saw earlier that the genetic and environmental patterns of influence on the 3Rs were rather similar to one another. What we knew from that research led her, and the rest of our team to expect that there would be both genetic and nonshared environmental influences on scientific achievement (but little shared environmental influence); that many genes and many environments, all of small effect, would be involved (the QTL hypothesis); and that there would be considerable genetic overlap between science achievement and other domains of academic achievement, although the relevant influential environments would differ (the Generalist Genes hypothesis). We were in for a surprise.

Dr Haworth began by exploring patterns of heritability in science performance, as rated by the twins' teachers at age 9, when the children were still in primary school (Haworth, Dale, and Plomin, 2008). Science did indeed seem to behave like English and Math, in that genes were the strongest influence and nonshared environmental influence outweighed the effect of shared environment. However, when she followed the children from primary to secondary school a surprising pattern began to emerge. By age 12 the influence of genes had decreased from a position in which they could explain 64% of the differences between children in terms of their science performance to one in which they explained only 47%

(Haworth, Dale, and Plomin, 2009). In other words, some genes had ceased to matter or were less effective than they had been, or an environmental factor or factors had become more powerful. Either way, science now appeared notably less heritable than the 3Rs. Even more surprisingly, the influence of shared environment, which we would have expected to virtually disappear around this age, had doubled: it now could explain one-third of the variance. In further research exploring scientific achievement at age 14 Haworth found that this pattern held true into the teenage years (Haworth, Dale, and Plomin, 2010). Science, it seems, behaves in rather a different way to English and mathematics during the high school years.

Haworth and the team began to consider and explore possible reasons for the changing pattern of heritability. One approach was to test the genetic correlation between science performance at age 9 and science performance at age 12. In essence, the genetic correlation would be 1.00 if exactly the same genes were influencing children's achievement in science at both ages and 0.00 if none of the genes affecting performance at age 9 were still influential at age 12. Typically, genes account for continuity and experience for change, so we would expect a strong genetic correlation. However, the genetic correlation between science performance at age 9 and age 12 for the TEDS twins was only 0.50. This means that only half of the genes influencing primary school science were still important to 12-year-olds in their high school science lessons. And, furthermore, the genes influencing science performance at age 12 were less influential than they had been at age 9.

So, what exactly is different about science at age 12 from science at age 9, and can it account for a lower heritability estimate at 12? One possibility is that the subject billed as science in primary schools is often not really science at all. Primary school science often involves the reading, comprehension, and retention of a factual text – a literacy task. It does not rely on (or even necessarily include) the hypothesis testing that lies at the heart of the scientific method, and is given less time than literacy and numeracy, and therefore a lower status. In this sense the "science" that is tested at age 9 might well be qualitatively different from the science we measure at age 12, and show more in common with literacy than with "real science." This could explain why genes have an equivalent influence on the two subjects at this age. If experimental, hands-on science was routinely taught to primary schoolers it is possible that the lower heritability estimate would show up then. This is unlikely to be the whole story, though, because analysis of data from the TEDS twins has shown that heritability estimates begin to decline at age 10, when children are still attending their primary schools.

We know from other research that enthusiasm for science dwindles during the primary school years and into early adolescence (Osborne, Simon, and Collins, 2003; Jenkins and Nelson, 2005). This, in combination with the surprisingly low genetic correlation, suggests the possibility that "science" as a named and tested subject should not be taught at all in primary schools. Schools could still introduce scientific subjects during topic work. If pupils do not enjoy a topic on, say, the human body or the solar system they will not then automatically discount the whole of science as being of no interest to them, or as something they're no good at.

Another option might be to teach "nature" as a subject and make it fairly practical in an observational rather than an experimental sense, leaving "science" to secondary schools with their labs and specialist teachers. It is possible that the slightly reduced heritability at the end of primary school reflects a move towards "real science" (although we still do not know why "real science" should be less heritable) but, given the declining enthusiasm that seems to start very early, it may still be best to leave science as a new and exciting area of learning for secondary school. It is one area in which it is possible for children not to be jaded before their high school career even begins.

Another possibility is that secondary school science education is at fault and is not nurturing natural potential effectively, is perhaps even suppressing genetic potential. If teachers were drawing out scientific potential effectively then maybe heritability would be higher. Perhaps the basic building blocks are not put in place securely enough? This hypothesis seems relatively unlikely, but our team plan to put it to the test in future research. One way of exploring this may be to carry out a genetically sensitive study of science achievement in a country where science is considered a greater priority for secondary education than it is in the United Kingdom.

And what of the increase in shared environmental influence? Well, we know that in TEDS the shared environmental correlation is 0.78, indicating that the environments that influence science performance at age 9 are, in the main, still effective at age 12, and that they appear to have even more influence for older children. This strong correlation leaves open the possibility that the home environment is more important than the school environment for scientific achievement, because this is the environment that is consistent across the two ages.

Identifying specific shared environmental influences on science achievement remains a tantalizing prospect for educationalists. Haworth recently explored the relationship between science achievement and the science learning environment (classroom and peers) when the twins were 14 (Haworth *et al.*, 2013). She found, like others before her, that there is a small correlation of about 0.20 between the science learning environment and science achievement. The most interesting result of this study, though, was related to the science classroom itself. We already know that most environments are subject to some genetic influence because of the process of genotype–environment correlation. This is where the environments experienced by an individual are affected by that same individual's genetic propensities. However, it was still surprising to find that genes influenced 43% of the differences between teenagers' experience of their science classroom, and that shared environmental factors could only explain 3%. Nonshared environmental influences explained 54% of the differences between our 14-year-old twins in how they perceived the environment in which they are taught science. In other words, the way in which young people perceive their classroom is highly subjective and influenced almost entirely by their own genes and their own experiences within it rather than the kind of objective measures that would typically be explored in any traditional assessment of classroom environment or educational quality.

Also, the correlation between science achievement and science learning environment, small as it is (0.20) turns out to be primarily driven by genes (56%) although shared environment does have some influence here (28%). This could mean that children who are naturally disposed towards scientific achievement are more positive about their science classes, and that children who are encouraged at home to do and understand their homework are also more positive about the experience than others. The questions we face are: What exactly is it about the experiences shared by siblings that could influence science performance? And, why would it be more important at ages 12 and 14 than at age 9?

One possibility is that the differences between environments shared by siblings increase after age 9. In terms of science this might mean that some children go to secondary schools with very good laboratory facilities and equipment while others go to schools that are less well resourced. It might mean that some go to schools that offer a general science qualification while others offer more challenging separate courses and qualifications in chemistry, biology, and physics. Given that these factors do not really come into play until secondary school level, they might well lie behind the greater shared environmental variance at ages 12 and 14.

Another possibility suggested by Haworth and her team is that genotype–environment correlations work in reverse when it comes to achievement in science. Normally the presence of genotype–environment correlations increases heritability estimates. However, if it is the case that children are being turned off science at quite young ages then they may not be seeking out scientifically enriching opportunities in line with their genetic potential. It is possible that if all secondary schools were equally well resourced, giving students the same amount of time to immerse themselves in science, equivalent facilities for doing so, and the same range of course and qualification choices, then shared environmental influence would be lower. It would be interesting then to note whether heritability or nonshared environmental influence would increase.

As we mentioned earlier, the home environment may play a key role. Given that the shared environmental correlation is so high at a time when pupils go through a major change in their education, home rather than school is likely to be the most consistent environment at play. In a home where science is discussed and where people fix things, discuss the plants and animals they observe on countryside walks, experiment, or model aspects of scientific inquiry in the kitchen, the garage, or the shed, children may be better equipped for the scientific opportunities available at school. This may represent a passive genotype–environment correlation in which scientifically minded parents pass on a scientifically stimulating environment to their scientifically minded children, say by having copies of *Nature* on the coffee table or letting them tinker with an old car; maybe getting out the chemistry or electronics kits once in a while and playing with them with their children. It might be an evocative genotype–environment correlation in which the child who gets excited by the rock-pools at the beach inspires a parent to spend ages there with them, find books about beaches and sea creatures at home, and plan another trip with more tools to allow more detailed exploration. Or it could be an active genotype–environment correlation in which interested children ask for science kits and metal detectors for Christmas, trips to science museums for birthday treats, and find opportunities for experimenting at home. For science, more than any other subject, measures of the home environment are likely to reveal a difference, and more research in this area is likely to be rewarded with interesting findings.

On the basis of what we do know we would advise some consideration of the possible merits of backing away from science as a subject until secondary school, when the time and resources to teach it well are available. In an ideal world, scientific resources would also be spread more equitably across all schools so that the experience of the scientifically minded child in an inner city school is as rich as that of the child in a high-end independent school. We would also recommend using topic work to encourage interest in scientific subjects at the primary school level without labeling them as "science." More research into why children's scientific motivation dwindles so fast would be a helpful precursor to designing suitable topic materials. We know from TEDS that boys report slightly more interest in science than girls even at age 9, so perhaps ways of engaging girls with these topics could be given special thought.

Differences Between the Sexes

This brings us back to sex differences in science achievement. It is well known that there are fewer women than men in scientific careers, and certainly fewer women than men in the top jobs in science. Only one-quarter of the US and European science and technology workforce is female, and the proportion of women working in "hard" sciences like mathematics and engineering is significantly lower than that. But how early are the seeds of this division sown?

By looking at scientific achievement in our sample Dr Haworth hoped to shed light on whether genes influence one sex more than the other in the years before pupils choose courses at age 14. In fact, what she found was that girls perform just as well as boys, and that they are influenced by the same genes and the same environments in equal measure. Roughly equivalent average performance in science has been found in the United States in the Nation's Report Card, and around the world in the PISA study. Girls and boys are not wired differently in terms of their scientific aptitude and achievement at ages 9 or 12. If there is a discrepancy between men and women in scientific careers (and there is: Steven Pinker calls it the "leaky pipeline") it is unlikely to be the result of genetic influences on ability or even of environmental differences at this early stage. If women do not pursue or succeed in scientific careers for either genetic or social reasons these must kick in during adolescence or adulthood. Given that genetic effects tend to be stable, it makes more sense to look for social reasons.

Given that the documented declining motivation for science is more marked for girls than for boys the discrepancy between men and women in the science workforce may reflect differences in course choice rather than differences in ability. Motivation has been shown to predict school course choice over and above grades. In other words, children pursue subjects they enjoy rather than ones they are good at.

Some developmental psychologists argue that the low number of women excelling in scientific careers is simply a reflection of the low number who want to pursue such a career in the first place. A recent study, for instance, found that people who are good at math and science – and also have strong verbal skills – are less likely to choose a STEM career (Wang, Eccles, and Kenny, 2013). The same study noted that the group with strong skills in both areas contained more women than men. There is an argument that, on average, women simply prefer to work with people rather than objects or abstract ideas. In the United States, even in the top 1% of mathematical ability, only one woman to eight men chooses a career in mathematics, engineering, or "hard" science. The other seven choose careers in medicine, biology, law, or the humanities, typically to work with, and to help, people. If women, even those with strong ability in science, choose not to become professional scientists because other opportunities are more attractive to them it is unreasonable to blame society or to label it discrimination. In this case it is not at all scandalous that women do not occupy half of the top jobs in science. What would be scandalous is if they were qualified for and wanted those top jobs but were denied them – something that has been true historically but, arguably, is not any more – or if girls were not given the same opportunities in school as boys, and in the world at large, to study science and to pursue it as far as they want to and as far as they can.

It is also pointed out regularly in the media that although average scientific ability is the same for both men and women, variance (the difference between the most and least able tails of the bell curve) tends to be greater for males than it is for females. What this means in practice is that more boys than girls will be terrible at science and more boys than girls will be scientific geniuses. For example, although the math averages of American teenage boys and girls are very similar, at the level of the most mathematically gifted there are 13 boys for every girl. Haworth checked the TEDS data to see whether the variance showed in scientific ability was greater for boys than for girls and found that it was (as it is for all cognitive abilities). At ages 9, 12, and 14 boys and girls perform equally well on average, but boys are slightly over-represented among both the most and the least able science students. Given that students in the upper tail of the distribution tend to pursue scientific careers this may also partly explain why we find more men than women working in science.

In Summary . . .

Behavioral genetics tells us that boys and girls tend to have equal scientific potential. It also seems that this genetic potential interacts differently with the science learning environment than it does in subjects such as English and math. Pinning down precisely why this is the case will have major implications for how the subject is taught. In the meantime, we already have enough data to suggest at least one hypothesis about optimizing scientific education in a developmentally and genetically sensitive way. We will discuss this further in Part Two.

References

Haworth, C.M.A., Dale, P., and Plomin, R. (2008). A twin study into the genetic and environmental influences on academic performance on science in nine-year-old boys and girls. *International Journal of Science Education*, 30 (8), 1003–1025.

Haworth, C.M.A., Dale, P., and Plomin, R. (2009). The etiology of science performance: Decreasing heritability and increasing importance of the shared environment from 9 to 12 years of age. *Child Development*, 80(3), 662–673.

Haworth, C.M.A., Dale, P., and Plomin, R. (2010). Sex differences in school science performance from middle childhood to early adolescence. *International Journal of Educational Research*, 49(2), 92–101.

Haworth, C., Davis, O. S., Hanscombe, K. B., Kovas, Y., Dale, P. S., and Plomin, R. (2013). Understanding the science-learning environment: A genetically sensitive approach. *Learning and Individual Differences*, 23, 145–150.

Jenkins, E.W. and Nelson, N.W. (2005). Important but not for me: Students' attitudes towards secondary school science in England. *Research in Science and Technological Education*, 23, 41–57.

Osborne, J., Simon, S., and Collins, S. (2003). Attitudes towards science: A review of the literature and its implications. *International Journal of Science Education*, 25, 1049–1079.

Wang, M. T., Eccles, J. S., and Kenny, S. (2013). Not lack of ability but more choice: Individual and gender differences in choice of careers in science, technology, engineering, and mathematics. *Psychological Science*, 24(5), 770–775.

Chapter 7
How do IQ and Motivation Fit In?

So far we have discussed genetic and environmental influences on school achievement, and along the way we have described the important finding that genes are generalists and environments are specialists. When, in time, we identify the particular genes that can account for individual differences in IQ scores we already know that most of them will also have a significant effect on academic achievement. This fits in neatly with what has been known and shown for many years, namely that IQ can reliably predict all kinds of success – academic, professional, social, marital, income, and even physical longevity (it turns out that people with higher IQs live longer) (Sternberg, Grigorenko and Bundy, 2001; Gottfredson and Deary, 2004). It is not overstating the case to say that IQ is the best single behavioral predictor of future success that we currently have. Even early ability levels can be reasonably strong indicators of later educational success, although IQ is not static and does change over time. The fact that an IQ score is such a useful and relevant statistic, combined with the fact that IQ can be improved environmentally,

G is for Genes: The Impact of Genetics on Education and Achievement, First Edition.
Kathryn Asbury and Robert Plomin.
© 2014 John Wiley & Sons, Inc. Published 2014 by John Wiley & Sons, Inc.

means that there is a place for IQ testing in personalized learning programs and genetically sensitive schools. However, as with DNA, people are often mistrustful of IQ scores and fear them as sources of discrimination rather than support. This, we believe, is because IQ test results are so often misinterpreted.

For instance, some schools use IQ tests for very young children but do not take into account the fact that IQ changes over the course of development and also that IQ can be taught. The practice is widespread in the United States where many schools, both public and private, attempt to identify gifted children at the age of 4. Hunter College Elementary School for example is among the most competitive and prestigious publicly funded schools in New York City and exists to educate "gifted" children. There are around 40 applicants for every place and the intrepid parents who apply on behalf of their children pay hundreds of dollars for them to sit an external IQ test. If the children score highly enough (in the top 2% of the population) they are invited to the second stage of the application process in which they will be observed in a group setting. The 50 successful applicants – 25 boys and 25 girls – who are admitted each year are then entitled to progress to Hunter College High School.

Since 2002 at least 25% of Hunter High's graduating classes have gone on to Ivy League schools. So acing the test and gaining a place at Hunter Elementary comes with pretty good odds of success later in life. And who doesn't want that for their child? On the one hand, the results vindicate the approach. If 25% of pupils are getting into top schools and achieving well then the IQ screen did a good job. On the other hand, if these really are among the most able 2% of children in the United States, and they are being educated in an enriched, accelerated environment, then why the hell do only 25% of them get into Ivy League schools? Shouldn't the statistic, even allowing for chance and human error, be much closer to 100%?

The mistake being made by schools such as Hunter College Elementary is not that they use IQ tests – this should be a good thing – but that they make false assumptions about the results. While there is no doubt that you can use an IQ test to identify a "gifted" 4-year old, IQ isn't static, and most children will score differently as they grow older and experience different environments. Some will improve, while others see their scores dip. But at Hunter College Elementary and other selective New York schools, both public and private, once a child has been identified as gifted they are entitled to keep that label throughout school, regardless of their subsequent performance. The apparent definitiveness of this single score is the problem. A child who does not make the cut at 4 years old is given no further opportunities to do so. The upshot is that gifted classes do not achieve the results you would expect them to achieve and children in "normal" schools and "normal" classes quite regularly outperform their "gifted" peers. There is a good genetic explanation for this.

Genes can explain roughly half, on average, of the differences between people in terms of their cognitive ability. The other half can be explained by nurture. That's on average though, and these figures repay closer scrutiny. Averages tell us little about individuals, and IQ provides us with a particularly neat illustration of this.

We have known for some time that the heritability of IQ – we will call it g (for general cognitive ability) as this is how the research we cite refers to it – changes over time in a clear and well-replicated pattern (e.g., Haworth *et al.*, 2009). What scientists around the world have found is that in the preschool years g is not very heritable at all. In fact genes only explain around 20–30% of the differences between preschool children in terms of g. A far more significant influence at this stage is the environment shared by siblings growing up in the same family, which can explain around 60% of individual differences between young children's cognitive abilities. The children who are being read stories, chatted to, shown how to play with developmentally appropriate toys, and introduced to their world in an informative, stimulating way do better than the children who aren't. Therefore, to a large extent Hunter College and its ilk are measuring the effects of the early home learning environment (and quite likely a private tutoring system) at least as much as they are measuring natural potential, and probably more so. The fact that the influence of the home learning environment wanes as children grow, and genetics comes to the fore, does a lot to explain why children who appear "gifted" at 4 do not necessarily look quite so gifted as they reach their teens. IQ testing should be carried out regularly in schools and used to support and inform a child's progress. A single score at age 4 might no longer be valid even by age 5. Also, IQ is not synonymous with achievement, merely one predictor of it.

When thinking about IQ, and especially high IQ, one's thoughts quickly turn to MENSA, the society for those with a talent for scoring very highly on IQ tests. MENSA describes its cognitively high-flying members thus:

> In education they range from preschoolers to high school dropouts to people with multiple doctorates. There are Mensans on welfare and Mensans who are millionaires. As far as occupations, the range is staggering. Mensa has professors and truck drivers, scientists and firefighters, computer programmers and farmers, artists, military people, musicians, laborers, police officers, glassblowers – the diverse list goes on and on.

It is clear from this, from everyday experience, and from highly reliable research studies undertaken around the world, that IQ and achievement are not the same thing. In fact, understanding the gaps between IQ and achievement can make a very useful starting point for personalizing each child's education. If they outperform their IQ what strategies do they use to do so? If they underachieve relative to their IQ, why might this be? This approach gives us a clearer understanding of a child's potential and of the internal resources they draw upon in school, be they cognitive or personality-based, than either can give us alone. Equating IQ scores with achievement is akin to believing that regardless of a driver's experience and skill the top spot in any motor racing contest will always go to the person driving the car with the biggest or most sophisticated engine. By this logic there's no point even having the race. Prizes should go to the engineers and mechanics but not to the drivers.

IQ and achievement are no more the same thing than car design and motor racing success. They're closely related; the best driver in the world would struggle to win the Monaco Grand Prix in a

Fiat Panda (unless that Panda were super-enhanced by a whole lot of nurture and perhaps a sprinkling of magic dust). But equally, the most powerful and sophisticated engine in the world, encased in the most beautiful, ergonomic racing car ever made, would be completely wasted on most of us. We would lack the personality, skill, training, practice, and instincts to drive it quickly enough or expertly enough to win a top-level race. Just as nature and nurture have a symbiotic relationship, so, too, do IQ and achievement. If IQ and achievement were the same thing, perfect predictors of each other, then they would correlate 1.00, a perfect correlation. In fact they correlate more like 0.50. For every child the relationship between IQ and achievement will vary in strength at different ages and stages. A great big chunk of school achievement is entirely independent of IQ. So, although IQ might be the closest thing learning has to an engine there's a lot more than engine power that goes into academic achievement.

Early enrichment programs such as Head Start in the United States and Sure Start in the United Kingdom are built on an understanding of the fact that IQ responds well to positive shared environmental influences in the preschool years. Pump-priming genuinely does work at this stage. Which is very useful if you want to coach your child into a place in a gifted classroom at age 4. They will reap the benefits for the rest of their school life, even if their cognitive ability later plateaus. Whether it is the best approach to giving underprivileged children the optimal start in life is a question fraught with difficulty, and one on which a consensus has not yet been reached. Head Start and Sure Start benefit preschoolers in genuine and concrete ways – improved cognitive ability scores – while they are still preschoolers but these measured effects seem to disappear not long after they start school. This highly disappointing but widely recognized finding can be partly explained by the changing heritability of g.

Children can be given an IQ boost at an early age but it doesn't last. However, an argument can be made that there are side-benefits to that temporary state of affairs that may have a more durable influence. The early years are perhaps best seen as a developmental window in which a positive enriched environment can outweigh the influence of genetic inheritance for a time. During that time young children can catch the learning bug and develop a taste for success before school, cynicism, and DNA, and the interaction between all three, really kick in. Our hypothesis would be that this can enhance motivation and whole-family attitudes to education and that this, in turn, will make a difference to children's experiences of school and to the likelihood of them fulfilling their personal potential. A long term follow-up study could perhaps find that early intervention is valuable not for long-term IQ or academic achievement gains but because it helps children vulnerable to failure to grow into adults living useful and happy lives, contributing to society and the economy when they might otherwise have proved a drain on it. We explore this further in Chapter 10, in the light of research conducted by a leading economist. Our research can, in some ways, explain why Sure Start and Head Start do not lead to long-term gains in objective markers of ability but we would be loath to recommend the cessation of programs which provide families and children with social support and pleasure, as well as learning opportunities, without looking at other tangible ways in which children, and society at large, may be benefiting from them.

But what about when children reach school age? If the influence of the shared environment is decreasing from this stage on, what purpose does school serve? At TEDS, we began to address this issue in a small way by asking what achievement, independent of cognitive ability, can tell us about how good a job a school is doing and how much value it adds to its pupils (Haworth, Asbury, Dale, and Plomin, 2011). When the TEDS twins were 12 years old we assessed them on a very wide range of measures, including ability and achievement, and then corrected (statistically) our measure of academic achievement for the effects of cognitive ability. Another way of putting this is that we looked at the bit of academic achievement that is not correlated with IQ. We wondered whether by taking IQ out of the equation we would show more clearly what difference schools actually make to the pupils who walk their halls.

One possibility was that achievement corrected for IQ would prove to be a "pure" measure of school quality, the extent to which schools "add value" to each child. This, of course, would require that all genetic influence on achievement is contained in the heritability of *g*, which was always unlikely. What we actually found was that achievement corrected for *g* is only slightly less heritable than before it was corrected. Genes still explain 40% of the differences between children in terms of their achievement, and these are different genes to the ones that influence *g* scores. Contrary to our expectations we found that achievement corrected for *g* showed even less shared environmental influence than before, dashing any hope that it might prove to be a marker of school effectiveness and that schools in themselves might act as effective shared environments. In fact nonshared environmental influence appeared to be significantly greater, accounting for over 50% of the differences between 12 year old TEDS twins in achievement test scores that had been corrected for the effects of *g*. In Chapter 9, we will discuss a study we have undertaken to explore what kinds of nonshared environmental influences might be found in schools. Possible candidates include relationships with peers and with teachers, enjoyment of classes, and positivity about school in general. We hope this line of research will show us the aspects of school life that make a positive difference so that we can start to design practical interventions to maximize their impact.

IQ + Genetics = Controversy (and Name-calling)

Underpinning this chapter is the fact – and it is a fact – that cognitive ability is subject to significant genetic influence, particularly as children grow into teenagers and adults. And herein lies one of the principal fault lines between geneticists and educationalists. The fact that cognitive ability is subject to significant genetic influence is a source of huge controversy. Even very well-informed critics worry that publicly acknowledging a tangible physical basis for individual differences in IQ may lead to discrimination against less able children. And yet, which of these people would deny that babies are born with different temperaments and that some children are more shy, daring, serious, or outgoing than others? Who could bring two children into the world and fail to recognize this from the outset?

It seems to us that the idea of genetic influence is not objectionable in itself, only when it is attached to traits that are emotionally loaded in our society – the bases of our discrimination. Therefore genetic findings that attach to intelligence, race, crime, or sexuality are always given a lot of (usually wrongheaded) coverage in our media; lines are drawn and tempers get frayed. When miscommunicated, the fact of genetic influence on ability appears to threaten reasonable political and moral debate. Genetic influence is all too often mistranslated as genetic determinism, and that way lies the madness of Nazi sterilization programs for those with a low IQ, and selective breeding programs for those at the opposite end of the spectrum. Such horrors of history are based on a willful distortion of science and have led to a widespread public mistrust of genetics in general.

The truth is that next to nothing is determined by genes, and our environments are hugely powerful. Ironically, one good way to illustrate this is to look at one of the many misguided schemes organized by genetic determinists. The program in question was a sperm bank for Nobel Prize winners. It was set up in San Diego around 30 years ago under the dry moniker of "Repository for Germinal Choice," later dubbed "The Genius Bank." The founder, Robert Klark Graham – inventor of the shatterproof spectacle lens – believed that "retrograde humans" were breeding to excess and that the only way to stop the harm this was causing was to set up a breeding program for the most intelligent. He began by collecting sperm samples from a very small number of Nobel Prize winners. This in itself proved to be an inauspicious beginning: old men's sperm isn't ideal for fertilization, however clever the donor. Graham then lowered his sights to successful, healthy MENSA members. Married women who themselves were members of MENSA were allowed to request a sperm sample; many have since reported that it seemed like a reasonable way of screening for good genes. So why was it misguided? Well, it was based on two false assumptions: first, that IQ and achievement are the same thing; and, second, that they are entirely genetic and will breed true, like Mendel's peas. As we have discussed throughout this chapter, environment plays a role in influencing IQ, and IQ alone does not predict achievement. For better and worse we are more complex organisms, with more complex behavior, than Mendel's peas. The idea was to generate a group of superbabies by making the process exclusive to those with high IQs. In this respect the project failed. Even with an egg from a high-IQ mother and sperm from a successful, healthy, high-IQ donor father, the program's 217 babies were born with a wide range of abilities and grew into children and young adults with an even wider range of abilities and achievements. IQ is not completely heritable and, anyway, is only one part of the achievement story. It is, nonetheless, a powerful predictor and, if used wisely, can help teachers to help children to reach their full potential.

This seems as good a place as any to reiterate that the science of genetics does not pose a threat to the education system. The genes for complex traits such as learning ability and IQ are never deterministic. Our aptitude for intelligence and achievement is not hard-wired and is subject to a panoply of experiences as well as to our unique genetic code. The understanding of a child's genetic inheritance, the possibility of which is only just beginning to emerge from research, simply helps us figure out which buttons to push to help realize that child's potential. Furthermore, even at the molecular level, genes do not behave in predictable ways; they can be switched off and on, or have their function or their volume altered by environmental experiences. This, again, undermines the idea that our abilities and behaviors can be predetermined. We'll say it one more time: genes are not deterministic. We need to move on and apply the many powerful truths of behavioral genetics to education.

Regular IQ testing can form an important thread as we observe a child's education from starting school through to leaving. It can help us to ensure that children who begin to underachieve can be spotted and helped back on track, and we can learn about strategies that result in overachievement.

Self-Confidence and Motivation

As we have said several times in this chapter already, IQ is just one predictor of achievement, albeit a strong one; there are others. Before genetic researchers became involved, a body of evidence had already been amassed showing that how good you believe you are at something – your self-perceived ability – can predict how good you actually are at it. If little Johnny thinks he's a great reader (whether he can sound out *Cat in the Hat* or not) he can improve his chance of becoming a great reader. We are currently finding the same pattern as we look at predictors of GCSE math grades among the TEDS twins.[1] This finding has been partly responsible for the "Good Job!" and high-self-esteem culture that has become prominent in the Western world. There is now a backlash against this culture; indeed, there is a compelling body of research, spearheaded by Professor Carol Dweck of Stanford University, showing that if you praise children too much, or in the wrong way, it can backfire. We will explore the considerable potential of Professor Dweck's empirically-based "mindset" philosophy in Part Two.

The current consensus among psychologists is that parents and teachers should praise effort rather than ability. In other words we should praise children who perform well by saying "That's brilliant; all your hard work really paid off!" rather than "That's brilliant; you're so clever!" Research with children of all ages – even toddlers – tends to show that children who are praised for ability rather than hard work become fearful of failure and nervous of taking risks, and that this in turn inhibits their progress. Praise for ability actually makes them less confident and less successful (Blackwell, Trzesniewski, and Dweck, 2007; Gunderson *et al.*, 2013). And yet there is a correlation between self-perceived abilities and achievement that has been found in many research studies including TEDS. So what lies behind a child's confidence in the first place?

Back in 1977 psychologist Arthur Bandura set out a hypothesis that our behavior is strongly influenced by the beliefs we hold

---

[1]   GCSEs are national exams which schoolchildren usually sit in year 11

about how capable we are and about how likely our efforts are to lead to the outcomes we want. He called them self-efficacy beliefs and claimed that they affect the choices we make, how much effort we put into pursuing our goals, and how much perseverance we show when faced with difficulties. There is an assumption, far more simplistic than those underlying Bandura's theory, that a child's belief in their own ability is the result of nurture and that if we tell children they're great often enough they will come to believe it and reap the benefits. It emanates from the widely accepted societal view that parents make children what they are, not by passing on their genes but by treating them in particular ways – the "blank slate" theory. Of course parenting is important, and there are a million reasons to be nice to your children and to teach them how to behave well and do what they can to succeed in life, but researchers are finding evidence of heritability everywhere all the time and this should change the way we think about child development. Parents are hugely important in myriad ways, but we are not as powerful in shaping who our children become as we have been led to believe.

Genetic researchers, including Dr Corina Greven working with our own team, have examined the assumption that self-confidence is the preserve of nurture, with surprising results which may help to explain why unbridled praise doesn't seem to have the desired effect. Firstly, Greven replicated existing research in showing that although g is the single best behavioral predictor we have of academic achievement, self-confidence also has a significant impact, and that this impact remains even when achievement is corrected for g.

More surprisingly, it turns out that 51% of the differences between the TEDS twins (when they were 9 years old) in terms of their self-perceived ability in academic subjects was explained by their genes. Self-perceived ability is at least as heritable as IQ and almost as heritable as achievement. It is not, it seems, solely a consequence of praise. Confidence genes seem to influence school performance both in conjunction with – and independent of – IQ genes, leading some to believe that in a roomful of equally bright and high-achieving people it is those who are self-confident who will go the extra mile. In fact scientists have now added self-confidence to the long list of traits for which specific genes are being sought. People are beginning to see self-confidence as something more akin to a personality trait than a fluctuating state of mind that can be altered straightforwardly by praise and encouragement. Hopefully, the genetic basis of self-confidence will, in time, help psychologists and educationalists to tailor interventions to boost self-belief, and in turn achievement, for individual children. It is likely that different interventions will be required for those who have a strong genetic predisposition to be self-confident than for those with the opposite. And just as IQ has a genetic basis but a person can be taught to perform better on an IQ test than they naturally would, the same is true of self-confidence. Someone who doubts themselves or their abilities can be given confidence training that will help them over particular hurdles. This is surely something that could form a valuable part of the school experience; we will explore exactly how in Part Two.

Improving Confidence and Cognition in the Classroom

So, what can we conclude about ability, self-confidence, genes, and education? And what difference can our conclusions make to teachers, parents, and educational policy makers? Well, to recap, IQ is a useful but not a perfect predictor of achievement; it is not very heritable when children are young but becomes increasingly so as they go through school and enter adult life. Achievement is also influenced by genes and this remains true when we remove the effects of IQ. Self-confidence predicts achievement to a lesser extent than IQ but is a significant influence nonetheless and, contrary to popular belief, it is influenced by nature as much as it is by nurture. So bright, confident kids tend to do well at school for both genetic and environmental reasons.

Research so far suggests that the effective aspects of school are those that are not shared by children growing up in the same family, that is, individual and individualized experiences. Identifying the school environments that pupils experience as individuals – and that make a difference to their performance – is a high priority for our team. We are currently conducting in-depth interviews with TEDS families in which identical twins are strikingly different to each other. The aim is to identify the aspects of the learning environment that really make a difference. However, while the research process takes time the lesson that these unique or nonshared experiences are the ones that make the difference is worth absorbing in itself and is something teachers can usefully focus on, over and above whole class or whole-school experiences, when planning each child's learning journey. Furthermore, the research suggests that personalized learning goals may be just as usefully targeted at outcomes like cognitive ability and self-confidence as they are at the more standard fare of academic achievement, such as reading, writing, mathematics, sport, and science.

Teachers must resist seeing IQ scores as markers of pure intelligence that override all other evidence: it is likely that the vast majority already do. Teachers should also be aware that IQ scores can be improved by coaching, and that some parents will provide this service for their children, meaning that results cannot necessarily be assumed to have come from a level playing field. This is especially true for matters such as entrance exams for private and selective schools. IQ scores are not a straightforward marker of ability, and furthermore they represent natural ability to different extents at different ages. However, any gap discovered between a child's IQ and their achievement may help with identifying the best buttons to push for their particular needs.

Perhaps it would be helpful to consider an IQ score (at an age where it has stabilized and genetic influence has come to the fore) as a "gift" but our ability to use it (to win top-level races with that big, sophisticated engine) as a "talent." In this view of things it is surely talent that counts. From a scientific point of view this makes a behavioral genetic study of over- and underachievement, in relation to IQ, a research priority. If we understand the genetic and environmental reasons why some children underperform while others overperform we have something that will allow us to tailor interventions to individual children, ways of planting them in soil that will help them to grow as fully as their natures allow.

And what about those educational establishments that allocate a specialized education to children based on the results of a one-off IQ test at age 4? Well, quite simply, don't do it. It's a waste of time, resources, and talent. The children with the highest IQs at age 4 will not necessarily be the highest-scoring ones at age 7 or 10. Wait until the children are older, or use IQ tests in a more regular and versatile way, and you will find that you accelerate learning for more of the right children, and that achievement rates will increase accordingly. The other argument, of course, is that selection is unnecessary if learning is truly personalized, and that not selecting makes space for excellence in children with mixed profiles.

This brings us on to the issue of "gifted and talented" programs in general. Usually "gifted" refers to high ability in academic subjects such as mathematics, whereas "talented" refers to high ability in nonacademic pursuits such as sports. The whole thing has become horribly politicized and attracted a lot of parental anxiety and social opprobrium in the United Kingdom. While some criticize the use of resources to help children who arguably need them least, others feel that exceptional children are ignored, and allowed to coast, while most input is given to children who might with an extra push meet national expectations and boost the school's ranking. Meanwhile, there is the whole separate issue of what happens to the children who struggle at the bottom end of the spectrum, and who have little chance of meeting national expectations.

All three groups are affected by the research on IQ and self-confidence in that the more they have of each, and the more tailored support they are offered to develop each, the better they are likely to achieve. It is our view – but this is a personal rather than a scientific perspective – that the bottom end of the spectrum should always be the highest priority when resources are limited. These are the children who need the most help to fulfill their personal potential; the children having to work hardest. But when resources are plentiful we should think in terms of individuals rather than groups to give each child a personalized education.

In conclusion, we would say that the development of IQ and self-confidence, as proven predictors of academic achievement, should form part of any good school curriculum. They are not exam subjects but they may markedly improve exam results as well as a whole host of other positive outcomes. The most viable mechanisms for enhancing pupils' cognitive abilities and self-belief will be those that are not shared by the whole class. Therefore, any sessions set up to enhance IQ or self-confidence will need to offer pupils the chance to choose from a range of activities and to make their own decisions about what they do and with whom they work. Improvement in these traits should, we hypothesize, mediate a positive relationship between learning environments and achievement. The teacher's role in these sessions may be more about observation and tracking than traditional teaching. The bottom line is that the education system can be improved if we use the school environment to maximize genetic potential in these two areas.

References

Blackwell, L. S., Trzesniewski, K. H., and Dweck, C. S. (2007). Implicit theories of intelligence predict achievement across an adolescent transition: A longitudinal study and an intervention. *Child Development*, 78, 246–263.

Gottfredson, L.S. and Deary, I.J. (2004). Intelligence predicts health and longevity, but why? *Current Directions in Psychological Science*, 13 (1), 1–4.

Gunderson, E. A., Gripshover, S. J., Romero, C., Dweck, C. S., Goldin-Meadow, S., and Levine, S. C. (2013). Parent praise to 1- to 3-year-olds predicts children's motivational frameworks 5 years later. *Child Development*, in press.

Haworth, C.M.A., Asbury, K., Dale, P.S., and Plomin, R. (2011). Added value measures in education show genetic as well as environmental influence. *PloS one* 6 (2), e16006.

Haworth, C.M.A., Wright, M.J., Luciano, M., Martin, N.G., De Geus, E.J.C., Van Beijsterveldt, C.E.M., … and Plomin, R. (2009). The heritability of general cognitive ability increases linearly from childhood to young adulthood. *Molecular Psychiatry*, 15 (11), 1112–1120.

Sternberg, R., Grigorenko, E., and Bundy, D.A. (2001). The predictive value of IQ. *Merrill-Palmer Quarterly*, 47 (1), 1–41.

Further Reading

Dweck, C. (2006). *Mindset: The new psychology of success*. New York: Random House. A popular account of Dweck's theory of fixed vs growth mindsets and how to develop them. For a slightly more academic treatment, try Dweck, C. (2000). *Self-Theories: Their Role in Motivation, Personality and Development*. New York: Psychology Press.

Plotz, D. (2005). *The Genius Factory: The Curious History of the Nobel Prize Sperm Bank*. New York: Random House. An entertaining and fascinating account of Plotz's follow-up of the babies born of the Nobel Prize sperm bank, the Repository for Germinal Choice.

Chapter 8

Special Educational Needs: Ideas and Inspiration

Given the importance of genes to learning ability and academic achievement it is unsurprising that having too much, too little, damaged or mutated genetic material can have a highly significant impact on how we develop. A child with Down syndrome, for instance, carries an extra copy of chromosome 21 – a case of too much genetic material. This extra chromosome is, with a relatively rare exception, found in every cell of the child's body. Because there has been a good amount of research into Down syndrome we now know that the extra chromosome 21 alters the way the child would otherwise have developed in some characteristic and predictable ways. Babies with Down syndrome are often recognizable from their facial features alone. They have almond-shaped eyes and small ears and noses. Looking closer, a parent or physician will often find a crease on the palm of the baby's hand, thickening at the back of the neck, and a gap between their big toe and their other toes. The extra chromosome also often leads to heart and respiratory problems, a tendency to hearing and vision deficiencies,

G is for Genes: The Impact of Genetics on Education and Achievement, First Edition.
Kathryn Asbury and Robert Plomin.
© 2014 John Wiley & Sons, Inc. Published 2014 by John Wiley & Sons, Inc.

low muscle tone, and anomalies such as teeth emerging in an atypical order. What is not obvious at birth is the way in which the extra chromosome 21, one of the smallest of our chromosomes, has impaired the child's ability to learn. All children and adults with Down syndrome have impaired learning. Even the most able person with Down syndrome is significantly less able, in terms of academic and cognitive ability, than they would have been without that extra genetic material.

There are over 1,000 genetic conditions, mostly less common than Down syndrome, which are also known to be detrimental to learning and cognitive ability. Children with Williams syndrome, for example, lack a series of genes on chromosome 7 – too little genetic material – and as a direct result have distinctive "elfin" features and can experience health problems such as narrowed arteries and raised calcium levels in infancy. Almost all children with Williams syndrome have a below-average IQ and many score well below the normal range. In Prader–Willi syndrome a handful of deleted genes on the copy of chromosome 15 inherited from the father (in most cases) can cause mental impairment, low muscle tone, hormonal imbalance, and very often an obsession with food.

Children with any of these genetic or chromosomal conditions can give us a valuable insight into the way that our genes work. For example, the fact that a slight alteration, addition, or reduction of our genetic information can affect so many aspects of our anatomy, physiology, and health emphasizes the extent to which genes are multi-taskers working in close conjunction with each other. As we discussed in Chapters 4 and 7, genes are generalists. It follows that close examination of the shared behavioral profiles of people with any one of these syndromes can teach us a great deal about genes and education.

These children are not the ones we have talked about in this book so far. They are genetically distinct from the normal distribution in terms of their ability to learn. Their learning difficulties are genetically caused, not just genetically influenced (although individual differences between people with a particular syndrome are likely to be influenced by genes and environments in the usual way).

Many of the conclusions we have drawn from behavioral genetic research, therefore, do not apply in the same way. Genetically sensitive studies of ability and achievement in Down syndrome, Williams syndrome, or Prader–Willi syndrome have not taken place because such studies require very large numbers of twins and adoptees; suitable samples are simply not available to us. However, although these children are not the focus of behavioral genetic research we write about them here for three main reasons. Firstly, any education system has a responsibility to consider the needs of all children; our conclusions about the personalization of education are as relevant to these children as to any others. Secondly, these particular children offer us a significant opportunity to look at individual differences that we know to have specific genetic etiologies. In doing so we have the chance to learn something about the implications of genetic differences, including the more fine-grained genetic differences to be found in the normal distribution, for education. And thirdly, we may well find some pointers in the existing specialist educational techniques applied to such children.

For the best part of two decades Professor Robert Hodapp of Vanderbilt University has blazed a trail for the taking of specific genetic causes of intellectual disability into account in education (e.g. Hodapp and Dykens, 2009). Special education classrooms, like mainstream classrooms, have often struggled to do this. Different genetic etiologies mean that children with Down syndrome, Williams syndrome, Prader–Willi syndrome, or any other diagnosed intellectual disability, have different needs and therefore should not just be lumped together as a single homogeneous group and taught in the same way as each other. Furthermore, children with learning disabilities are likely to need different approaches from their teachers than children with emotional or behavioral disabilities, or children with profound and multiple needs. The genetic anomalies that make these children different from the general population also make them different from each other, and this has important implications for their optimal education.

Children with Down syndrome for example have been found to show a specific pattern of strengths and weakness in relation to learning. As a group (and, as always, individuals will often differ from the average or norm for their group) they have a tendency to do better with tasks involving visual rather than auditory processing. So, when teaching a child with Down syndrome, it is important to do a lot more showing than telling. This understanding has led to educational interventions that appear to have very good results. For example, children with Down syndrome are very likely to be delayed in the area of language development. This makes sense when you consider that auditory processing is a specific weakness for many of these children. We learn to speak by listening to and gradually engaging with the verbal stimuli around us. But guess what helps? Teaching the child to read, ideally as young as possible. Because children with Down syndrome often respond well to visual stimuli, teaching language through the written rather than the spoken word makes sense. And some children who have been taught to read early have been shown to have age-appropriate reading levels, significantly higher than their IQ, a strength that could bolster self- and peer-esteem in the school environment as well as having a beneficial effect on the child's language skills.

Children with Williams syndrome, by contrast, are believed to have a strength in speech and language skills relative to their IQ. Their ability to communicate verbally is usually somewhat stronger than their visuo-spatial capacities. When educating children with this particular disability it is therefore better to present as much information as possible verbally rather than visually. For those with Prader–Willi syndrome, sequential processing – say, remembering a series of numbers or hand movements – can be particularly difficult, and such children are better at simultaneous processing. This means, for instance, that learning to count is best done using words in conjunction with real objects.

The different ways in which these groups of children learn are largely driven by their genetic profiles, and each child will develop more quickly and more fully if this fact is taken into account. Children with Down syndrome who are taught verbally will, on average, develop more slowly than they otherwise could, and children with Williams syndrome taught using visual props may also fail to thrive. Children presented with learning approaches that do not work for them are likely to become frustrated and disaffected, compounding their learning difficulties. To make matters even more complicated we are talking about averages for each of these groups here, but the children need to be considered as individuals too.

Personalization is complex and, although group profiles can steer it, the needs of the individual, rather than the average for a group, always have to be the focus. However, the fact is that teachers in special education face a situation in which they might have a handful of children who learn visually and a handful who learn verbally, as well as other children with a whole host of other highly particular needs and challenging behaviors. The challenge to educate each of these children in the way that will draw out the best that they have to offer is considerable. Special education teachers know better than anybody that standing at the front of a classroom and delivering a single lesson with the aid of a piece of chalk or even an interactive whiteboard is rarely if ever going to work. As a result, special education teachers, because of their experience with children with known group profiles, are likely to have very good advice for the rest of us about personalizing education.

However, even in special education, where genetically influenced individual differences are writ large and are therefore better understood than in mainstream schools, there is a degree of despair about personalizing education effectively. Professor Hodapp describes a resistance to taking into account the different genetic etiologies of intellectual disabilities when lesson planning for fear of what has been termed the "Balkanization" of special education. In this scenario, administrators fear that separate classes will be required for children with different disorders and that it will become, frankly, an administrative nightmare. This, in a nutshell, is what all resistance to personalized learning – in both special and mainstream schools – is about. We don't have a good enough understanding of how to do it, and to many it seems impossible. True personalization may make genetic sense; it may be the best way to nurture each child's potential; it may even make for the ideal educational system; but how can it possibly be put into practice? It's a fair question, and it is the first one that we will begin to answer in Part Two of this book.

The Expansion of Special Educational Needs

Our discussion of special educational needs so far has focused on children with genetically caused learning disabilities, but these are not the only children under the coverage of the special needs umbrella. In the United Kingdom, parents can apply for, and be awarded, a *statement* – a legally binding document that lays out the extra support that their child needs and has a right to expect. Statemented children make up 2.7% of the UK school population. The children we have focused on thus far would usually be obvious candidates for a statement, although in some areas – and especially during budget cuts – their parents may, rather disgracefully, still have to fight for it. A statement may lead, for example, to a mainstream school being given money to provide the child with a one-to-one helper. When this works well, the helper can personalize the child's education by taking the class teacher's lesson and presenting it in a way that is in tune with what they know about the individual child and about the disorder that has led to their statement. The success of the approach is dependent on hiring people with the ability and will to personalize in this way, and providing training so that they can keep up to date with new methods of supporting such children. This approach can work very well for learning disabilities and for behaviorally based special educational needs such as autism and ADHD. A statement is also a requirement for a child to be offered a place in a special school.

A child with no diagnosis who is not making adequate progress in school can also be considered to have special educational needs. When this happens in the United Kingdom at the moment – although the system is currently in the process of a major overhaul, which may withdraw the support these children need – the school will put the child on the first tier of special educational needs classification, which is currently called School Action. At this level, parents are informed that their child is not progressing in a particular area; an Individual Education Plan is drawn up, and the school puts extra help in place to support the child to make adequate progress. This might involve extra tuition, equipment, or basically anything that the school feels might make a difference. If the child still fails to make enough progress they are moved to School Action Plus, in which the school approaches outside professionals such as speech and language therapists, physiotherapists, counselors, or psychologists. In some instances School Action Plus is appropriate as the first port of call.

This system, when it works, is a good approach to personalized learning. A teacher spots that a child needs help and tries to provide what they need for as long as they need it. What is quite interesting is that the approach has led to estimates that as many as one in five children in the United Kingdom have special educational needs, a figure that has generated a somewhat hostile backlash. One example, which has been cited in a rather sneering fashion in the press, relates to children in one school being placed temporarily on the special educational needs register because their fathers were fighting in Afghanistan. But should we really sneer? If anxiety about their fathers fighting in Afghanistan was interfering with the children's ability to learn then it is difficult to understand why offering them extra support is a bad thing. Their special educational needs are real and likely to exist only temporarily. Once again, it is the labeling that causes the problem. It is the urge to classify and define – to call anybody "special" – that seems to encourage others to extend their claws.

And what of the other end of the spectrum, those labeled as "Gifted" and/or "Talented"? Is high ability a special need? Are these children an educational priority? Is this taking pandering to the ambitious middle classes a little too far? Or is it a way of meeting the needs of bright children that benefits them and all those around them by not segregating them in selective schools? Are the brightest children in our schools genetically different from the normal distribution? Do they perhaps have extra or deleted genetic material that scrambles their DNA blueprint in a more cognitively fortuitous way than Down syndrome, Williams syndrome, or Prader–Willi syndrome?

Well, we have already shown in TEDS that high g is affected by the same genes as the rest of the normal distribution and that the same is true of high ability in English and math. However, it may be that if we assessed only the very highest-ability children (the top 0.1% rather than the top 5 or 10%) we might find something different going on. It's not possible to carry out such assessments with our research design because of the large samples required; even though we have a very large overall sample it is still not large or statistically powerful enough when we eliminate 999 of every 1000. However, on the basis of what we do know, the most able children in a school have the same genes as everyone else. But does it matter that the work being set for the majority of the class is too easy or too boring for them? Well of course it does. If the relatively slow pace of the class impairs a bright child's ability to learn then that is a problem that needs addressing and, yes, the child has a special educational need for more stimulation, appropriately tailored to their own profile of strengths and weaknesses. Just like their classmates.

When "gifted and talented" children are added to the current SEN mix we're probably looking at one in four children having special educational needs. In our opinion, this number is still far too low: it shouldn't be one in four or one in five, but five in five. In our view, all children experience special educational needs at some point. Their difficulties may be temporary or permanent, caused by genes or environment, but they deserve an immediate, sympathetic, personalized response for as long as it takes to address the problem. Some of these children may need a statement of some sort to protect their right to an effective education, but most need no sort of labeling whatsoever. In an ideal world, what they need is for the school to have a documented profile of their strengths and weaknesses, including any genetic information available at that time. This information could then be combined with knowledge of the particular problem being experienced by the child to work out the type of help required. If we take away labeling and begin to think just in terms of getting extra support for all children as and when they need it then the special educational needs debate loses much of its heat. For genetic reasons all children will find some ways of learning, subjects, or experiences difficult. If they are carefully tracked, monitored, and understood, then extra help can be provided so that problems can be solved and children do not get stuck with negative beliefs about their own ability, or unnecessarily low achievement. Quite often children are referred to as "being" special needs. No child "is" special needs but every child is likely to "have" special needs at some point in their education. We discuss ways of meeting these special educational needs in Part Two.

Personalized Learning in Action

Many families with young children with major diagnosed additional needs come into contact with the Portage service, an approach to personalized learning named after the Wisconsin town in which it was developed. Children are assigned a Portage visitor who visits them regularly in their own home. During the first few sessions the Portage worker will observe the child and, together with their parent(s) or carer(s), will go through a developmental checklist that has been broken down into tiny steps. They mark each milestone the child has already achieved and then use this information to set a baseline on which to build, a developmental profile that is often uneven or "spiky," as it reflects the child's actual development across a range of areas.

At this point the Portage home visitor will set named goals for the child to work towards over the next few months. Each visit they will introduce toys and activities to help the parent support their child in achieving these goals. The system is based on finding out what a child can already do and building on this, rather than focusing on what they can't and remedying it. The baseline represents the child's own unique and often uneven developmental profile rather than that of the average 1-, 2-, 3-, or 4-year-old with (or without) their particular diagnosis. In Chapter 14, when we discuss what personalized learning might look like in a genetically sensitive school, we will draw some lessons from this insightful approach to guiding all children to fulfill their own unique potential.

In Summary . . .

The very fact that the special educational needs system exists tells us that children with specific requirements cannot be taught effectively with a single method. Instead they must be offered an education that is more focused on them, taking into account their genes and their particular learning profile. We believe there is a lesson here for mainstream education, where children are too often treated as if they are all exactly the same. They are not. Thanks to genetic and environmental influences, all children have special educational needs of one sort or another at one time or another. Impractical though it may appear to be, mainstream schools need to provide a similarly personalized approach to their pupils. That's the theory. In Part Two we'll attempt to put it into practice.

Reference

Hodapp, R.M. and Dykens, E.M. (2009). Intellectual disabilities and child psychiatry: looking to the future. *Journal of Child Psychology and Psychiatry*, 50, 99–107.

Chapter 9

"Clones" in the Classroom

So far we have mainly focused on the effects of genetic influence on achievement, ability, and disability. Now we turn our attention to the environment, in particular the learning environments that children are exposed to in their schools. We ask how much difference does what goes on within a school or a classroom really make. It should be a no-brainer, but it isn't.

By 2005, after exploring the 3Rs and Science over the course of several years in TEDS, we had found no statistically significant relationships between the school environment and academic achievement, and it wasn't for lack of trying. We had asked thousands of children, parents, and teachers about class sizes, school buildings, resources like books and computers, chaos in classrooms, and a whole host of other oft-cited factors and yet, when we fed their ideas into genetically sensitive studies, these factors did not add up to a hill of beans. That is to say, they accounted for almost none of the differences between our children in terms of their achievement. The environment within a school, it appeared,

G is for Genes: The Impact of Genetics on Education and Achievement, First Edition.
Kathryn Asbury and Robert Plomin.
© 2014 John Wiley & Sons, Inc. Published 2014 by John Wiley & Sons, Inc.

had no impact on children's academic performance. This finding drove us nuts. It drove us, in time, to write this book. But first of all it drove us to try a little bit harder. Maybe our measures weren't sensitive enough? Maybe we were missing something?

We already knew that the important influences were likely to be nonshared and that the cleanest way of identifying nonshared environmental influences is to look at differences between identical twins. So that's what we decided to do. By using identical twins we can control for genetic effects; if there is a difference in their achievement it has to be caused environmentally.

Around this time Professor David Almeida, a psychologist from Pennsylvania State University, came to visit. Professor Almeida is an expert in diary studies. Instead of asking people to answer one-off questions about themselves he asks them to report regularly (daily or even several times a day) on their activities, thoughts, and feelings. He believes that the experiences that really cause problems in life are the little, niggling, cumulative ones, the ones that grind you down. His diary method captures the stress lurking in people's everyday lives, and he is fond of quoting a remark attributed to Chekhov: "Any idiot can face a crisis – it's day-to-day living that wears you out."

Professor Almeida usually conducts his research with middle-aged people coping, to greater and lesser degrees, with the responsibilities of work, parenting, mortgages, health problems, bills, and caring for their own ageing parents. Unsurprisingly, he finds plenty of stress with which to work. In discussing our problem with him it occurred to us that perhaps his diary methodology would allow us to get closer to young people's experiences of school than the questionnaires we had used so far. Also, in an age in which we are told that childhood stress is on the rise, it would allow us to look at the impact of stressful experiences in school. Maybe a more in-depth approach would allow young people to identify the aspects of the school experience that we were missing, the magic that makes school work.

Together with Professor Almeida we designed a diary measure of the school environment to send to our identical twins. We began to feel a little more optimistic. Our plan was to begin by talking to a sample of 50 or so pairs of identical twins every school day for two weeks. We planned to ask them the same questions each day and then analyze the data to see whether their answers correlated with their teachers' reports of their achievement.

We started by devising the measure we would use for our daily diary interviews. We began with a series of questions about peer-related stress at school, including: "Did you argue with a pupil in your class today?" and "Were you excluded or left out of anything by someone today?" We then moved on to academic pressures: "Did you struggle to understand something in class today?"; "Did you fail to hand in some homework that was due today?" We also prepared a list of questions about relationships with teachers: "Did your teacher call on you to answer questions today?"; "Did your teacher tell you off today for not listening in class?" Although we felt that stress was a potentially important aspect of the school experience that had not been looked at in a genetically sensitive study before, we also wanted to focus on the positive side of formal education in a new way. For this we used the psychological concept of "flow."

"Flow" was first described by psychologist Mihalyi Csikszent-mihalyi, and is a measure of how engaged we are in the activities we undertake. To some extent it is a measure of happiness, at least for the duration of the activity in question. Csikszentmihalyi describes a person "in flow" as being deeply involved in an activity they find enjoyable; not being bored; and not having to make any effort to concentrate. He designed a "Flow Questionnaire," which opens with three quotations: one from a rock climber, one from a composer, and one from a dancer, all along the following lines.

> My mind isn't wandering. I am not thinking of something else. I am totally involved in what I am doing. My body feels good. I don't seem to hear anything. The world seems to be cut off from me. I am less aware of myself and my problems.

After reading these quotations respondents are asked whether they have experienced similar feelings and which activities prompted them (Csikszentmihalyi and Csikszentmihalyi, 1988). By doing this they identify their own "flow" activities, which can be as extreme as rock climbing or as mundane as washing the car. They then answer a series of questions about the "flow" activities they have identified. We decided to adapt Csikszentmihalyi's questionnaire for our study and defined English, mathematics, and science lessons as potential "flow" activities. We planned to ask the twins in our study about how "in flow" they had been in these lessons each day by asking to what extent they agreed with a series of "flow"-related statements, e.g. "I get involved"; "I get anxious"; "I knew exactly what I was meant to be doing"; and "I got bored."

Finally, we planned to finish our daily diary interviews with a rather rough and ready single-question measure – because this was a pilot study, a good place to try things out. We would simply ask the twins which number between 1 and 10 best described their day at school if 1 was the worst day they could possibly have and 10 was the best.

Once the measure was ready and had been tested for feasibility on a small sample of children our interviewers began to phone around a socially representative sample of TEDS families with 10-year-old identical twins to ask if they would like to take part. The response was positive, typical of the ongoing generosity of the families in our study. Over a two-week period our interviewers spoke to 60 or so pairs of twins every evening after school, and asked their teachers to rate them in terms of their achievement in English, mathematics, and science. Responses were fed straight into our database and we waited on tenterhooks, hoping for a clear sign of how the environment within a school works to influence achievement (Asbury *et al.*, 2008).

It didn't come. It is fair to say that on the first day we worked with our exciting new dataset we were more than a little disappointed. There were signs here and there of experiences that looked as though they might matter, at least a little bit, but there was no Eureka moment. That said, when we returned to the data with our tails between our legs and our expectations lowered we found little hints of gold in the otherwise murky river.

The first glint came from the fact that although peer, academic, and teacher stressors did not appear to be associated with achievement in general, they were negatively associated with children's "flow" and their positivity about the school day. Stress at school appeared to be negatively linked with happiness at school. The correlations between peer and academic stressors and "flow" were statistically significant. It wasn't what we had set out looking for, but it was a start.

What we were especially interested in, though, was finding statistically significant correlations between differences in school experience and differences in achievement within an identical twin pair. Because both children in an identical pair share all of their genes, any differences between them have to be caused environmentally. If differences in their experience correlate with differences in their achievement it means that the experience in question works as a nonshared environmental influence. We were working from the assumption that school should be packed to the rafters with nonshared environmental influences on most aspects of behavior, but especially achievement.

We did find some statistically significant correlations. Firstly, we found that if one identical twin experienced more peer stress than the other, that same child was less likely to report being happy, engaged, and "in flow" during their English lessons. However, although the child with more peer group difficulties was less happy in English classes this did not necessarily mean that they performed less well. Neither identical-twin differences in peer problems or "flow" correlated at a statistically significant level with identical-twin differences in English achievement. This finding might have come about because the teacher ratings we used were too blunt to capture small differences; because our sample was too small to capture statistically significant correlations; or because there really is no link. For instance, our teachers gave us ratings of, say, 3, 4, or 5 when, in reality, pupils are assessed as being at a Level 3A, B, or C or 4A, B, or C and pupils are expected to improve by approximately two sublevels per year. In practice, this means that if one twin is a 4A and the other a 4C one is working a whole year ahead of the other, and yet our data could not capture this. That said, even with the significant limitations of a bluntness to our teacher ratings and a small sample size, the correlation between differences in peer stressors and differences in English achievement actually came very close to achieving statistical significance and, for this reason, will remain in the melting-pot for the bigger study we plan to carry out next. We are cautiously optimistic about finding a statistically significant relationship between peer problems and achievement.

Next we found that identical twin differences in peer stress did in fact correlate significantly with identical-twin differences in mathematics achievement, with the child who experienced more problems performing less well in math. Also, identical-twin differences in "flow" in science lessons correlated significantly with identical-twin differences in science achievement. This research suggests, albeit very tentatively, that helping children to manage their relationships and their feelings about any problems within those relationships (easier said than done of course), and finding ways of really engaging them in lessons, particularly science, may turn out to have a measurable effect on achievement, independent of the DNA each child brings to the table. This is vague but promising, something for us to work with.

In more recent research we have been talking to parents of identical twins aged between 16 and 18, trying to account for differences in how well they performed at GCSE. It is worth noting that we do not see many major differences between identical twins' examination results, confirming our findings at younger ages that genes are highly important in the development of academic achievement. However, we do see some, indicating important environmental influences, and the families concerned often mention the peers hypothesis. For instance, we spoke to the parents of one pair of 17-year-old identical twin boys, Daniel and Mark (not their real names). Mark achieved 10 A*–C grades in his GCSEs and was studying A-Levels [1] and aiming for a university place to study music technology. Daniel on the other hand managed four GCSEs with A*–C grades, went to college to do a vocational course, but

[1]   A-levels are national exams linked to university admission, usually taken in year 13.

failed the first year and was unemployed and seeking on-the-job training. These are highly significant differences in achievement that are likely to have major influence over differences between the boys' experiences of adult life. In fact, the differences are already beginning to show, although not necessarily in the ways we would expect. Mark is experiencing more stress and isn't going out much because he's worried about not keeping up in class, whereas Daniel is spending a lot of time at the gym and enjoying an active social life. When we spoke to their parents their first response was just that Mark put in more effort and it paid off. "Daniel spent too much time messing about, being the classroom clown." And yet, the presence of a stronger work ethic in one twin than the other still remains to be explained.

When we discussed differences in Daniel and Mark's experiences and their achievement in a little more detail we found out that the boys were in separate classes throughout school, providing ample opportunity for nonshared experience, and in the first couple of years seemed to be doing equally well. By the end of primary school, however, Mark was regularly outperforming his brother. When asked to think about this a little more their parents quickly turned to the effect of friendships. Although Daniel and Mark were "best friends from being born" and had some friends in common they generally moved in very different circles and "It's all about the company you keep." They describe Mark's friends as kids who were motivated and intelligent, whereas Daniel's friends were fun-loving and not too worried about meeting expectations. This is just one example and, as others have pointed out, the plural of "anecdote" is not "data." However, the facts remain that many parents worry about the impact of negative friendships on their children, and our pilot study has highlighted peer relationships as a potential source of nonshared environmental influence on academic achievement. In terms of genetics Daniel should have been able to achieve everything that Mark has achieved but something – and friendships are one possibility – stopped him. There has been some behavioral genetic research into friendship, and also bullying, and it seems like a good idea to bring this research into the educational context and think about what, if anything, can be done to help young people to make and maintain healthy friendships that may have a positive impact on their success in school.

Positivity and Achievement

Finally, our crudest measure – rating the day overall on a 1–10 scale – came up trumps. Identical-twin differences in average day-rating were correlated at a statistically significant level with identical-twin differences in mathematics and science achievement. Put simply, the twin who was more positive about school did better in math and science. There is of course the chicken-and-egg possibility that the child doing better in lessons was more positive about school, but the relationship is interesting nonetheless.

So, by the end of our study we were left with the hypotheses that positivity about school, "flow" in the classroom, and peer stress, work as nonshared environmental influences on achievement. We also saw significant relationships between peer and academic stress and "flow"; and, in some subjects at least, between "flow" and academic achievement, which suggests a possible chain-reaction. We also saw that stress was negatively associated with "flow," suggesting the hypothesis that classroom stress is linked to low morale and that this low morale, in terms of "flow" and positivity, has a negative knock-on effect on academic achievement. Perhaps there would be merit in teaching children how to handle stress and achieve "flow" as a means of boosting their academic performance? Such "thinking skills" could prove to be a powerful part of the curriculum – an idea we examine further in Part Two.

Clones in the Classroom

One of the most striking aspects of this study, which replicated previous studies, was that identical twins in the same classroom had different experiences within it and different perceptions of it. If you think about this, it really is quite astonishing. These children are, genetically speaking, clones of each other and yet, even when raised in the same family and educated in the same classroom, they experience the world differently. Even with the short two-week period in which we studied them, these twins perceived their experiences to be different from those of their co-twin. Far from correlating 1.00 they correlated less than 0.50 for peer stressors and relationships with their teachers. The same was true of their "flow" in science lessons, where they correlated only 0.36, suggesting that enjoyment of science lessons (and relationships with peers and teachers) is more heavily influenced by nonshared experiences than it is by either genes or the shared environment. Identical-twin correlations for academic stress, "flow" in English and mathematics classes, and positivity about school (average day-rating) did not exceed 0.50 by very much either. By contrast, identical-twin correlations for English, mathematics, and science achievement were all around 0.80, suggesting a much stronger role for genes and, possibly, shared environment on achievement than for perceptions of experience.

How does one child come to perceive (or objectively experience) more problems with schoolwork and relationships than their genetically identical co-twin – to all intents and purposes their clone? Chance has to be a contender. Also, environmental differences beginning at conception – position in the womb, access to the placenta etc. – may set identical DNA packages on their way into diverging universes where every choice and experience enhances each twin's individuality. What we see in the data, though, is that school does act as a nonshared experience, at least subjectively, and as such may influence behavior, personality, and lots of other traits. However, we are not a great deal wiser about whether and how it influences academic achievement. This requires serious consideration and exploration given that, as the title of a well-known book on the subject tells us, children in much of the Western world spend a minimum of *Fifteen Thousand Hours* of their childhood in compulsory education (Rutter, Maughan, Mortimore, and Ouston, 1979). On a personal level, if you think over your own experience of education what evidence of nonshared environmental influence do you see? We predict that most people will see a great deal. Were you inspired by a particular teacher? Did you get a great part in the school play that opened up doors for you? Did you feign illness to stay at home because you were bullied in school? Did your best friend leave the school or ditch you? There are opportunities for nonshared environmental influence on every school corridor and in every school classroom. The challenge is to pin down how they work and their areas of particular influence. As we mentioned earlier, we've taken up this challenge in a new study, again talking to identical twins and their families, in which we aim to figure out the aspects of education that really make a difference to the achievement, wellbeing and decision-making of young people as they prepare to leave school.

References

Asbury, K., Almeida, D., Hibel, J., Harlaar, N., and Plomin, R. (2008). Clones in the Classroom: A daily diary study of the nonshared environmental relationship between monozygotic twin differences in school experience and achievement. *Twin Research and Human Genetics: The Official Journal of the International Society for Twin Studies*, 11 (6), 586.

Csikszentmihalyi, M. and Csikszentmihalyi, I.S. (1988). *Optimal Experience: Psychological Studies of Flow in Consciousness*. New York: Cambridge University Press.

Rutter, M., Maughan, B., Mortimore, P., and Ouston, J. (1979). *Fifteen Thousand Hours*. Cambridge, MA: Harvard University Press.

Further Reading

For a further example of talking to the families of identical twins in order to generate new ideas about how the environment works see:

Asbury, K., Dunn, J., and Plomin, R. (2006). The use of discordant MZ twins to generate hypotheses regarding nonshared environmental influence on anxiety in middle childhood. *Social Development*, 15, 564–570. This paper looks at influences such as bullying and traumatic events around the birth as possible predictors of anxiety.

Chapter 10

Mind the Gap: Social Status and School Quality

Somehow, working-class kids have been cast as both the heroes and the villains in the media's education fairytale. On the one hand there are the few who, in spite of being born and brought up in relatively inauspicious circumstances, get scholarships to selective schools or places at Oxford and Cambridge, Harvard and Princeton – the rags-to-riches stories. Cinderella anyone? Newspapers like photos of these kids almost as much as they like photos of bouncy girls in short skirts waving around their notifications of successful exam results – and that's saying something. On the other hand, many more of these kids don't get good exam results, and the schools they attend are precisely the schools that ambitious middle-class parents are moving house to get away from. Newspapers profess themselves saddened and scared by the photos they choose to print of these young people – usually spotty youths with menacing expressions and hoodies (not the Little Red Riding Hood kind). They are often smoking, pregnant, or both. Find a school that has been designated as failing and you can bet your

G is for Genes: The Impact of Genetics on Education and Achievement, First Edition.
Kathryn Asbury and Robert Plomin.
© 2014 John Wiley & Sons, Inc. Published 2014 by John Wiley & Sons, Inc.

bottom dollar it isn't situated in a leafy suburb, nor populated by the sons and daughters of teachers, doctors, lawyers, and accountants. And when the discussion is narrowed to boys, as it so often is, we're pretty much exclusively in the realm of baddies. Working-class education is, it seems, a slough of despond characterized by low aspirations, low income, low status, and nascent lowlifes.

So what's really going on? Is this impression that does so much to drive the hype about school choice actually a fairytale or just fair and accurate reportage? Do children brought up by parents with few or no educational qualifications, low occupational status, and low income in a tricky neighborhood necessarily do badly at school, and if so, why?

Answering these questions brings up some complicated and uncomfortable truths. The first of these is that socio-economic status (SES), which in this context usually refers to parents' educational qualifications and occupational status, is as good a predictor of academic achievement as IQ (with which it is also correlated). This has been shown in studies all over the world. In spite of all the emphasis on school quality, as measured by Ofsted in the United Kingdom, SES leaves it trailing in the dust when it comes to predicting how well children will achieve in school (Walker, Petrill, and Plomin, 2005). Humble beginnings, it seems, are often associated with lowly outcomes.

The second uncomfortable truth is that SES is partly heritable. Genes can explain approximately half of the differences between people in the educational qualifications they gain, and 40% of the variability in the status of the jobs that they do. It sounds odd to say that an aspect of a child's environment, such as their family's social status, is influenced by genes but really it is unsurprising when one considers genetic influence on academic achievement and how this has to feed into educational and occupational status. We also know that genes can explain 30% of income differences, sometimes included in measures of SES. Other categories of SES have also been proposed based on economic capital (wealth assets), social capital (the people you associate with) and cultural capital (the books you read, concerts you attend, museums you visit etc). There has been no genetically sensitive study of these additional aspects of SES, but we predict that they are likely to show even greater levels of heritability as they capture more of an individual's achievements, proclivities, and preferences. Given that parental SES is heritable, and that children's academic achievement is also heritable, it is not especially surprising that genetic research has found the links between SES and achievement to be partly mediated by genes. In sum, SES is influenced by genetic as well as environmental factors and this, for many, represents an uncomfortable truth.

Furthermore, in the United Kingdom the social class gap for achievement is one of the widest in the developed world. On the face of it this evidence is depressing. Kids born to low-status parents seem to have the deck stacked against them. Both genes and environment are working against them and their families. They are massively over-represented in estimates of children currently labeled as having special educational needs. The gap between them and their middle-class counterparts is evident long before they start school and it only widens over time. By the same token, though, we know that environmental factors influence SES at least as much as genetic factors and that the environment can be used as an agent for change. We also know that some pupils from low-SES families achieve very high levels of academic success, and we suggest that an important way forward for research is figuring out how and why these children are able to do so well. If we can answer that question we will have more power to promote the environmental influences that make a positive difference to children and young people from economically and socially disadvantaged backgrounds. We will be able to identify new ways of reducing inequality and drawing out potential, by working with rather than against children's genetic makeup.

Behavioral genetic research cannot turn the observable evidence on its head; SES really does predict achievement, partly for genetic reasons. What behavioral geneticists can do, though, is dig a little deeper to uncover the particular genetic and environmental influences at work, and begin to understand how they might work together. It is worth noting here that there is a general consensus that education is the best mechanism for equalizing opportunity and promoting social mobility. However, some recent sociological work (Goldthorpe, 2012) suggests that the story might not be as simple as this. We may need to look beyond schools for the environmental factors that influence SES and social mobility, and that might be involved in positive genotype–environment correlations. Children learn at home as well as at school, and personalizing all learning environments is likely to enhance genetic potential.

Low SES: What Does It Look Like?

We begin by trying to describe a small part of what it means to label a family as low-SES; and how the experiences of such families are likely to differ, on average, from those with higher social status. Who hasn't watched a posh politician talking about "the underprivileged" on the news and wished for some genuine, non-cartoonish understanding of the complexities and contradictions involved in people's lives?.

A working-class family is likely to be poorer, in terms of money coming into the house, than a middle-class family. This relative poverty can affect all aspects of a home environment and has an impact on the children growing up in it. A recent UK study, for example, found a strong and significant effect of income poverty on cognitive function in 5-year-olds (Schoon, Jones, Cheng, and Maughan, 2012). Low income, we know, has knock-on effects, including parental stress and a lack of resources to pay for extras such as swimming or music lessons, educational trips and out-ings, IT equipment, books, and sports kit. Children growing up in income-poor families therefore do not experience equality of opportunity in this regard. This is true throughout their educa-tion, so they are less likely to be exposed to resources such as private tutors when they struggle with a subject, constraining their achievement and their future prospects. While stress is certainly not the sole preserve of low-SES families, the resources we mention are routinely available to well-off children, affording them more chance to develop and find their talents. It is no coincidence that the pony-club set tend to look and sound very middle class and are not usually the children of cleaners, call-centre workers, or the unemployed. Equalising these opportunities may represent one way of leveling the playing field. It is worth noting though that equalizing environments will not decrease heritability estimates. On the contrary, as we argued in Chapter 3, heritability can be seen as an index of equality. When the environmental playing field is level then genetic differences between individuals will be more, not less, visible. In Chapter 1 we made a case that this seems, at worst, a small price to pay if all children are receiving equal opportunities to fulfill their potential. At the moment, children from low-SES families do not experience equal opportunities: that is a problem we can perhaps do something about, to the benefit of disadvantaged children and young people.

Research has shown that, as well as being poorer, children in low-SES families are talked to less than children in higher-SES families, and often start school with significantly less linguistic knowledge (Purcell-Gates, McIntyre, and Freppon, 1995). Parents in working-class families, on average, spend less time with their children and are less responsive to their needs than better-off, more educated parents. This could reflect lack of time, an excess of stress, or a different approach to parenting, but it does appear to be linked with their children's cognitive development. A genetically sensitive study of this phenomenon could tell us more about how the link works. This finding has led some researchers in psychology and economics to advance the argument that disadvantage is more about a lack of stimulation than a simple lack of financial resources. This is one avenue for future genetically sensitive research. For instance, a home-based Portage-like service, currently only offered to preschool children with diagnosed special educational needs, could perhaps be offered to children in disadvantaged families. Portage home visitors could focus on modeling useful ways of stimulating child development through play and communication. The benefits of this could be assessed in an experimental trial.

Other aspects of the home environment that have been shown to have a negative impact on cognitive ability and school achievement – and that are more commonly found among low-SES families – are chaos and crowding (Melki *et al.*, 2004). The US Census Bureau considers homes occupied by more than one person per room to be crowded, and in 2000 more than 5% of US households met this criterion; according to the 2001 UK Census, the figure in England and Wales was 7%. By this definition a home with a living room, kitchen, bathroom, and two bedrooms is crowded if it is occupied by six people or more, but is adequate for a couple with three children. Even after controlling statistically for the effects of SES, children from crowded homes were found to experience high levels of stress, behavior problems, and delayed cognitive development. We also know that parents in crowded homes are less responsive to their children. Researchers have hypothesized that this may reflect adults unintentionally withdrawing from their children as they try to cope with constant and noisy demands for their attention. A recent study (Evans *et al.*, 2010) showed that residential crowding in early childhood can predict cognitive development at 3 years of age and that the link was largely mediated by mothers not responding very well to their children. We know that parental responsiveness matters and that crowding is harmful to children, in both the home and day-care settings.

Chaos is related to crowding, and to SES, but research has shown that chaos predicts academic achievement even when the effects of SES have been controlled for. The children who do well at school tend to come from relatively quiet, orderly homes with predictable routines. It has been shown that children in noisy, chaotic, disorganized homes tend to withdraw from academic challenges and show low expectations and low levels of persistence with their schoolwork (Brown and Low, 2008). The more chaotic children perceive their homes to be, the poorer their performance in school.

A recent and genetically sensitive study of this phenomenon asked whether the correlation between chaos and achievement is mediated by genes or by the home environment. This research, carried out by Ken Hanscombe of the TEDS team, started from the premise that genes influence achievement but that they might also influence children's subjective perceptions of the level of chaos in their own homes. This turned out to be true. When we asked our 12-year-old twins about chaos in their homes and families, identical twins gave more similar responses than non-identical twins, suggesting that perceptions of the home environment were influenced by genes. This led to a hypothesis that nature as well as nurture may perhaps mediate the relationship between chaos and achievement. Analysis of the data confirmed this hypothesis. Two-thirds of the relationship was mediated environmentally and one-third genetically. The environmental influence here makes intuitive sense. A child in a chaotic home may not have a quiet tidy space in which to do their homework, or may not have been supported in establishing a routine for getting it done. They may not be able to find the books and other resources that they need when they need them. They may be tired if they do not have a consistent bedtime routine and may not be able to concentrate because of fatigue or because the noise of the TV or of shouting makes it difficult. But how does the genetic part work? Well, we don't exactly know, but we suggest that it is very likely to depend on whose genes are mediating the link between high levels of chaos and low levels of achievement, something we will explore in future research.

So, if the parents' genes are to blame then we have an example of passive genotype–environment correlation. Parents who create chaotic home environments may not encourage high achievement in school and may not take an interest in homework, at least partly because of a genetic predisposition not to do so. Their children will be at risk from both the genes they inherit from these parents and the non-educational environment they create. However, given that the children in this study were 12 years old and attending high school, it seems unlikely that their own genes are not implicated to some extent. In this case we may be seeing an active genotype–environment correlation in which if children are uncooperative about going to bed, turning off the TV, or sitting down to work, then their parents may give up trying to impose structure, and teachers may have to spend more time on managing their behavior than on actually teaching them. Either or both genetic pathways make intuitive sense and further research is needed to fully understand how the genetic link between chaos and achievement actually works.

So far, we have seen how the home environment – and SES in particular – can have an impact on a child's achievement at school. But how can this be counteracted by a genetically sensitive education system? In Part Two of this book, we will propose a radical new way to bridge the divide between home and school – one that could perhaps help inform the way that teachers interact with individual pupils, and encourage better practices at home by focusing on equal opportunities. It is a method that takes into account the reality and power of genotype–environment correlations in order to improve children's levels of engagement and motivation. We think it could ease the burden on teachers and boost the achievement levels of otherwise vulnerable children. Some of the inspiration for this approach will be discussed later in this chapter.

What Does the Heritability of SES Mean?

So, SES is influenced by genes as well as experiences, and the relationship between SES and achievement is partly genetic in origin. The two things are linked by a person's DNA. This means that the children of parents who themselves did not succeed at school and went on to achieve low status in society are likely to resemble their parents as much for genetic reasons as for environmental reasons. In essence, it is likely that children growing up in low-income families – the families targeted by projects like Sure Start and Head Start – are genetically as well as environmentally vulnerable. The question facing us, therefore, is what can be done to support the more vulnerable members of society, to promote social mobility on the far left-hand-side of the bell-shaped curve where it is most sorely needed? We don't have definitive answers, but we can make some tentative suggestions; and we can state unequivocally that this is a question in need of an answer. We have seen that there are many ways in which disadvantaged children are not exposed to equal opportunities, a phenomenon that is manifestly unfair.

One way to tackle the problem of some families getting stuck in a low-SES rut may be to focus on equalizing opportunities for the most vulnerable families. However, it is worth reminding ourselves that while this may have a very beneficial effect it will not reduce heritability estimates for either SES or achievement. Rather, access to new opportunities might nurture natural potential that would otherwise have lain dormant.

Experiencing an environment that is impoverished, either literally or figuratively, because of parental status is unfair and stands in the way of maximizing individual as well as social and economic potential. Therefore, low-SES families should be prime candidates for extra resources and carefully targeted interventions. And to an extent they have been given them – in the form of programs such as Head Start in the United States and Sure Start in the United Kingdom. However, these initiatives are vulnerable because of their failure to make lasting changes to children's IQ levels, and this is of particular concern in a time of global recession and widespread funding cuts. Also, it can be argued that these programs do not actually manage to access the most vulnerable families either at the right time or in the right way. Indeed the groups run by Sure Start, although often excellent, are also often full of middle-class mums and their babies, while the disadvantaged families they are designed to help are in the minority.

Notwithstanding these problems, solutions for which can be found, the strategy of investing in young children as a means of leveling the playing field and improving life-long outcomes for disadvantaged children has been championed by Nobel Laureate and University of Chicago Economics Professor James J. Heckman. Heckman is interested in what he calls the origins and remediation of human inequality. In one of his many articles on the subject he states that:

Investing in disadvantaged young children is a rare public policy initiative that promotes fairness and social justice and at the same time promotes productivity in the economy and in society at large.

(Heckman, 2006.)

Heckman uses economic arguments to support the theory that we under-invest in preschoolers. He has described a series of core concepts for social policy in early childhood, all of which make genetic sense. The first is that genotype–environment interplay influences brain architecture and skill formation. In other words, the dance between genes and experience makes a difference to developing brains, which are very plastic and particularly susceptible to environmental influence in early childhood. Secondly, skill mastery follows hierarchical rules. Basic skills have to be mastered before the next level of skill can be approached. This concept lies at the heart of our recommendations for education in Part Two. Thirdly, skills are interdependent and affected by experience. And fourthly, there are sensitive periods when the brain is most plastic. Heckman's four concepts fit neatly with our behavioral genetic finding that shared environmental influence has most impact in the preschool years.

We have already touched on the problem that Head Start and Sure Start are considered failed projects in some quarters because they do not improve IQ in the long term. However, Heckman argues that this interpretation misses the bigger picture. To illustrate his case he refers to the Perry Preschool Program. This was a two-year experimental intervention carried out in the early 1960s for 3- and 4-year-old disadvantaged African American children identified as being at risk for school failure. It was a case-control study in which the subjects attended nursery for $2\frac{1}{2}$ hours every weekday morning and once each week had a $1\frac{1}{2}$-hour afternoon visit from their teacher at home. This was designed to involve the mother in the educational process and to help to implement the preschool curriculum at home. The children learned through play rather than formal instruction, and the focus was on developing noncognitive skills. By age 10 the case children's IQs were no higher than those of the control children. However, their achievement test scores were significantly higher because, argues Heckman, they were more motivated to learn. This is interesting given that achievement shows higher heritability than cognitive ability (and genotype–environment correlations are often hidden within heritability estimates). The program had no long-term effect whatsoever on IQ, but the effects on achievement and wellbeing were significant. These children were followed up at age 40 and the treated group had higher rates of high school graduation, higher salaries, higher percentages of home ownership, were in receipt of fewer welfare benefits, and had fewer criminal charges than the controls (Schweinhart et al., 2005). In sum, they had higher SES than the controls, and their new and improved SES is what will predict their own children's achievement, rather than the social status they were born into: social mobility in action. There is no doubt that their genes still resembled those of their parents but the environment was used in a way that appears to have given them a leg up, provided them with new experiences with which their genes could interact in a positive way.

Behavioral genetic research supports Heckman's argument that the best time to invoke shared environmental influences to affect children's achievement, perhaps via their self-confidence, motivation, and aspirations, is before school begins. From this point onward the influences of shared environment tend to diminish. We can also say that one correlate of SES which shows promise for improving the chances of disadvantaged children is sensitive, responsive parenting and that preschool initiatives can usefully focus their attention on this, as was done in the Perry Preschool Program. Interventions in which educators bring education into the real-world home environments of disadvantaged children may seem expensive, but the evidence suggests that, over the course of a life, they might pay for themselves. Nurturing natural potential in the preschool years needs further consideration as a strategy for promoting social mobility and drawing out individual potential.

School Quality

Failing schools are usually situated in deprived areas. Therefore, school quality is inextricably linked with SES. In the United Kingdom this problem has led to a policy of competition and the marketization of education in which parents are given choice, or at least the illusion of choice, about the school their child attends. Researchers uniformly conclude that this has been a rather unsuccessful solution to the inequality problem. In fact it actively works against closing the social gap because the middle classes have been shown to have greater purchasing power and more ability to "play the game" in successfully applying to the school of their choice – whether that involves moving house, hiring a tutor, becoming more visible in church, saying the right things on a form, or developing a child's talent for sport or music. The same conclusion has been reached in research that has looked into the issues of school choice, school quality in relation to pupil demographics, and achievement according to SES background. The bottom line is that, in this instance, diversity of opportunity actually appears to exacerbate inequality of opportunity – a cautionary tale which reminds us not to be too gung-ho or generalist with our recommendations for a genetically sensitive education system.

In reality there has not been a great deal of genetically sensitive research into school quality as an environmental influence. However, there has been a lot of nongenetically sensitive research on this subject, which concludes that school quality may be a red herring that has little or no causal relationship with academic achievement. So, when a school is named and shamed as "failing" because pupils are failing to succeed academically it does not necessarily follow that this failure is entirely the fault of the school *per se*. If the same school were filled with pupils from high-SES families with a genetic predisposition towards academic achievement it is highly unlikely that, even with no changes whatsoever made to the staff or the curriculum, the school would qualify as "failing." However, although the circumstances may be difficult, it is clear that these schools for deprived communities are not succeeding in their task of educating their pupils well.

The landmark Coleman Report, published in 1966, was a massive, 700-page, exploration of educational equality in the United States. Coleman, a sociologist, concluded that pupil background and SES was far more important to achievement than differences in school resources. The report suggested, contrary to current expensive UK approaches such as the Academies and Free Schools programs, that throwing money at schools and increasing blanket per-pupil spending would not make a whole lot of difference, and that interventions should be targeted at families rather than at schools. In TEDS we, too, have found that school quality explains only a tiny proportion of the differences between children in terms of achievement, and that SES at the family level is the heavy hitter in terms of influence (Walker, Petrill, and Plomin, 2005).

Coleman's report does leave room for teacher quality to contribute to individual differences in achievement even though resources don't – a lead supported by economic as well as psychological and sociological researchers (e.g., Hanushek, 2010). Teacher quality tends to be variable even within a school, something that any parent watching their child go through consecutive classes in a single school will recognize. Also, it is likely that even the very best teachers are not similarly effective for all children and that genotype–environment correlations are at play here unless the teacher is completely sensitive to individual needs and leads a fully personalized classroom. This, of course, is the ideal and the more we strive to achieve the ideal the closer we will get. The evidence from nongenetic studies suggests that teacher quality matters significantly more than quality of school buildings or resources, or complex admissions arrangements. The message coming forward is that interventions focused on active learning between parent and child, and teacher and child, are the most promising.

Proximal processes between adults such as teachers and parents, and the children they teach and nurture, are the most fertile ground for genotype–environment correlations to flourish and for children to learn in an environment that recognizes their needs and their strengths. SES matters, and this has to be addressed in any equitable education policy. School quality doesn't matter all that much but the interface between genes and experience, between a mother and her language-learning toddler, or a teacher and her math-averse student, really does. These lessons are drawn from educational, economic, and sociological research as well as our own field, and will be borne in mind as we design our own version of a genetically sensitive education system that offers equal opportunities to all pupils.

The take home message is that although socio-economic status *does* predict school achievement and *is* influenced by genes, building interventions around environmental influences that negate the effects of poverty, reduced stimulation, crowding and chaos is the best way forward if we are to create equal opportunities for all.

References

Brown, F.D., and Low, C.M. (2008). Chaotic living conditions and sleep problems associated with children's responses to academic challenge. *Journal of Family Psychology*, 22, 920–923.

Evans, G. W., Ricciuti, H. N., Hope, S., Schoon, I., Bradley, R. H., Corwyn, R. F., and Hazan, C. (2010). Crowding and cognitive development: The mediating role of maternal responsiveness among 36-month-old children. *Environment and Behavior*, 42(1), 135–148.

Goldthorpe, J.H. (2012). *Understanding – and Misunderstanding – Social Mobility in Britain: The Entry of the Economists, the Confusion of the Politicians and the Limits of Educational Policy*. Oxford: Barnett Papers in Social Research. http://www.spi.ox.ac.uk/fileadmin/documents/pdf/Goldthorpe_Social_Mob_paper.pdf (accessed 25 June 2013).

Hanushek, E.A. (2010). The Economic Value of Higher Teacher Quality. NBER Working Paper Series, Working Paper 16606 http://www.nber.org/papers/w16606 .

Heckman, J.J. (2006). Investing in disadvantaged young children is an economically efficient policy. Presented at the Committee for Economic Development/The Pew Charitable Trusts/PNC Financial Services Group Forum on "Building the Economic Case for Investments in Preschool" New York, January 10, 2006.

Melki, I. S., Beydoun, H. A., Khogali, M., Tamim, H., and Yunis, K. A. (2004). Household crowding index: a correlate of socioeconomic status and inter-pregnancy spacing in an urban setting. *Journal of Epidemiology and Community Health*, 58(6), 476–480.

Purcell-Gates, V., McIntyre, E., and Freppon, P. A. (1995). Learning written storybook language in school: A comparison of low-SES children in skills-based and whole-language classrooms. *American Educational Research Journal*, 32(3), 659–685.

Reynolds A.J., Temple J.A., Ou S., *et al.* (2007). Effects of a school-based, early childhood intervention on adult health and well-being: A 19-year follow-up of low-income families. *Archives of Pediatrics and Adolescent Medicine*, 161(8), 730–739.

Schoon, I., Jones, E., Cheng, H., and Maughan, B. (2012). Family hardship, family instability and cognitive development. *Journal of Epidemiology and Community Health*, 66(8), 716–722.

Schweinhart, L.J., Montie, J., Xiang, Z., Barnett, W.S., Belfield, C.R., and Nores, M. (2005). *Lifetime Effects: The HighScope Perry Preschool Study Through Age 40*. Monographs of the HighScope Educational Research Foundation, 14. Ypsilanti, MI: HighScope Press.

Walker, S.O., Petrill, S.A., and Plomin, R. (2005). A genetically sensitive investigation of the effects of the school environment and socio-economic status on academic achievement in seven-year olds. *Educational Psychology*, 25(1), 55–73.

Further Reading

For more information on Ken Hanscombe's genetically sensitive research into the nature and nurture of family chaos we suggest the following two papers: Hanscombe, K. B., Haworth, C., Davis, O. S., Jaffee, S. R., and Plomin, R. (2010). The nature (and nurture) of children's perceptions of family chaos. *Learning and Individual Differences*, 20(5), 549–553; and Hanscombe, K. B., Haworth, C., Davis, O. S., Jaffee, S. R., and Plomin, R. (2011). Chaotic homes and school achievement: a twin study. *Journal of Child Psychology and Psychiatry*, 52(11), 1212–1220.

For a different take on the implications of relationships between genes, social status and achievement Charles Murray's book makes for an interesting read: Murray, C. (2008). *Real Education: Four Simple Truths for Bringing America's Schools Back to Reality*. New York: Three Rivers Press.

Chapter 11

Genetics and Learning:
The Big Ideas

Behavioral geneticists have found out a great deal more about learning and behavior than it is possible to cover in this book. We have chosen to concentrate on the strongest findings and those most relevant to school achievement. Together they can be distilled down to seven powerful principles – the "Big Ideas" of this chapter's title. It is upon these principles that we will attempt to build a genetically sensitive education system in Part Two.

Big Idea #1: Achievement and Ability Vary, Partly for Genetic Reasons

This fact lies at the heart of all our research. If we identify an average (mean) g score or an average score in an English, Mathematics, or Science examination, 50% of the population the test was designed for will fall above that score and 50% below it. The fact that these abilities are normally distributed means that people will differ both upwards and downwards of the average score to predictable degrees. Even when we improve the average we do not reduce the differences between people (known statistically as the variance). Our DNA has a moderate to strong influence on where we, as individuals, fall within the distribution. Too many educational policies consider all those who score below the mean as "failing"; this is a fundamental misunderstanding of both the statistics and the biology involved. If national education systems do not acknowledge this fact, and take it into account, they will continue to waste money and human potential on approaches that make no difference whatsoever to individuals or to society. Acceptance that achievement and ability vary, partly for genetic reasons, has to be the foundation for a better school system. It is the job of schools, once all children have been trained to an acceptable level, to nurture this diversity; there is no point trying to make all children achieve the same score in everything.

Big Idea #2: The Abnormal is Normal

We will never find a single gene that can explain a person's ability (or lack of ability) in reading, writing, mathematics, science, sport, or, for that matter, depression, obesity, conduct problems, or asthma. Human behavior is influenced by many genes and many experiences, each of small effect (the QTL hypothesis). They combine in myriad ways to affect who we are and what we do. We will never be able to engineer brilliance or failure by switching particular genes on or off here and there because the impact would be different in different people, depending on the entirety of their allelic and experiential history.

The QTL hypothesis tells us that low ability in any academic subject, including reading and mathematics, is not genetically distinct from ability in the normal range or at the high end. The genes that affect the mathematical ability of a mathematics professor and a young person struggling to pass a basic mathematics exam are the same, albeit not necessarily in the same versions (alleles). This makes an enormous difference to how – and whether – we diagnose special educational needs, at the levels of both struggling and gifted children. It also affects how we tailor education for such children and how we spend our resources. If a well-conceived educational intervention was targeted only at the least able children, for example, it could close the gap between the two tails of the bell curve a little, while not affecting the population average a great deal.

Big Idea #3: Continuity is Genetic and Change is Environmental

Behavioral genetics studies so far suggest that the genes affecting achievement or ability at one age, say 7, will continue to affect achievement or ability at all later ages (this is less true for science as it is currently taught than for other subjects). In principle this means that if genes alone were involved (as genetic determinists would have you believe) we would be able to take test results from young children and predict their test scores in adolescence and adulthood with great reliability. We could also use them to predict a whole range of other life-outcomes. Because continuity is genetic, it is true that we are likely to gain predictive power from genetic information – this is why we need to think so hard about emerging biotechnology and the possibility of a Learning Chip – but the success rate of prediction will always fall significantly short of 100% because the environment, acting on the individual and through interplay with their genes, acts as an agent for change. If a child who has previously been performing well in school begins to perform uncharacteristically poorly the causes are almost certain to be environmental. Dramatic fluctuations in schoolchildren's performance or behavior should be treated very seriously indeed in order that their social causes may be identified and either rectified (if the child's achievement and behavior are suffering) or encouraged and learnt from (if the child's achievement and behavior are showing improvements). Just as plants develop differently in different climates, or under the care of different gardeners, so, too, do human beings. Understanding genes and relying on the continuity of their effects allows us to focus on the relative unpredictability of influential environments and the way in which they can work constructively with a child's genetic makeup.

Big Idea #4: Genes are Generalists and Environments are Specialists

The evidence of behavioral genetics tells us that the same genes are involved across a wide range of cognitive abilities and achievements. Thinking about g can help us to understand this concept. If we return to g as a measure of our cognitive firepower we hypothesize that, in time, the genes that influence g will also be shown to influence academic achievement in, for example, reading, writing, and arithmetic. Research is already beginning to bear out this theory. If it were only genes that were involved, ability profiles would be more uniform across the board than they currently are.

The fact that environments are specialists is momentously important to schools and teachers. While some experiences can draw out and enhance (or damage) potential in a particular subject, say science, we have no reason to believe that the same experiences should have the same effect in mathematics. There is no single, hallmarked way of educating children. Different school subjects, not to mention different children, call for different techniques. Educationalists, be they parents or teachers, have the power to maximize genetic potential. But they need to find and press the right buttons in order to do this, and to allow pupils sufficient freedom to identify their own buttons.

Big Idea #5: Environments are Influenced by Genes

Our understanding of gene–environment interplay will develop exponentially over the next few decades. We are seeing interesting progress, for example, in fields such as epigenetics – the study of how chemical changes to DNA can alter gene expression without affecting the genetic code. However, what we know already is that our experiences are affected by our genes through the process of genotype–environment correlation. Environments do not operate independently of our genes but rather in conjunction with them. Equally, genes do not operate independently of experience and therefore educationalists need not fear genes as being deterministic. Instead, teachers should think of themselves as drawing out a child's genetic potential rather than writing haphazardly on a mythical blank slate.

One particularly exciting avenue for research and, in time, intervention, is the area of active genotype–environment correlations. This is where individuals select their own environments on the basis of genetically influenced traits that can mediate the relationship between an environment and an outcome, such as personality or temperament, IQ, motivation, or self-confidence. These are the most likely reasons we find environments to be heritable (the nature of nurture) and we predict an understanding of these processes will lead to greatly enhanced personalization in schools. We hope our own research team will be able to make a major contribution to these developments.

Big Idea #6: The Environments that Matter Most are Unique to Individuals

We know that the most important environments, particularly after the infant and toddler years, are those that are either objectively unique to an individual or which may be shared by siblings growing up in the same family but affect each of them differently. We have shown how even genetically identical twins brought up in the same home and taught in the same classroom by the same teacher perceive their learning environment differently, making subjective and individual experiences particularly important when we consider new ways of using schools to draw out potential and personalize each child's learning environment. As ever, the focus needs to be on the individual child – the child, not the problem – and what works for them. When we ask how heritable a wide range of educationally relevant behaviors are we usually find that nonshared experiences explain the majority of the nongenetic variance. It is now a research priority to pin down which particular experiences make a difference, and for which children.

Big Idea #7: Equality of Opportunity Requires Diversity of Opportunity

Would a world in which we were all treated exactly the same way be a utopia? Let's say we all get to live in large, pleasant homes on wide, tree-lined boulevards; we are all sent to versions of the same highly respected and high-achieving schools; and our family incomes are equalized. Will we all become more similar? The answer is not really. There may be some superficial similarities brought on by a shared lifestyle, but 50% of the population will still be more high-achieving and cognitively adroit than the other 50%. Certain behaviors, including achievement, may be boosted for the population as a whole but the shape of the bell curve would not change very much. Those on the low-achieving left-hand-side would still be pretty much as far away from those on the high-achieving right-hand-side as they currently are, although some of the changes we suggest may, we hope, close the gap at least a little. And, furthermore, the equalization of experience would lead to higher estimates of heritability than we currently have. If nurture is the same for everyone it can no longer drive differences between people: only nature can do that. By introducing more choice into education we believe we can create schools in which more natures can be fully nurtured.

In Part Two we put these Big Ideas into practice in the form of a series of testable policy ideas, and we propose one version of a genetically sensitive school. But first we look at some of the techniques already available to those interested in personalizing education.

Part Two
In Practice

Chapter 12

Personalization in Practice

OK, so you're an experienced teacher of 30 pupils, only slightly jaded by the constant trickle of government edicts about what you should do and how you should do it, and still basically happy with the career you chose all those years ago. It's Friday afternoon and you're whistling cheerily in anticipation of the weekend ahead as you pack your bag and do some last-minute tidying up in the classroom. And then the Principal pops in. Alarm bells ring immediately; the Principal never just "pops in." This time is no exception. She wants to let you know that she's agreed to trial a new approach in which you and your colleagues will be regularly observed and assessed on the basis of how effectively you personalize the teaching and learning environment in your class.

She smiles as though she's presenting you with a large bouquet of orchids as she tells you that she would like to see your "personalization improvement plan" on her desk by half term, which is in just two weeks. You smile and you nod and you say "No problem.

G is for Genes: The Impact of Genetics on Education and Achievement, First Edition.
Kathryn Asbury and Robert Plomin.
© 2014 John Wiley & Sons, Inc. Published 2014 by John Wiley & Sons, Inc.

Have a great weekend!" all the while unleashing a torrent of abuse in your head.

The next half hour passes in a blur of hair pulling (your own), moaning with the teacher in the next room, and eating the biscuits you'd managed to ignore all day. You're already doing your best. What on earth do they want from you? You appreciate that it probably would be great if you could teach 30 different lessons at the same time, but how on earth are you supposed to do that? What can you actually do about the fact that Danny Hardcastle is bored to tears by how easy he's finding math but can't take on anything harder until you find time to show him some new techniques; that Millie Bracken still can't read much and is getting teased by the other kids for reading baby books; and that blue table are winding each other up to the extent that none of them have made any progress in anything for weeks. Every time you focus on one problem it seems to create several more. You trudge out of school with a heavy heart, already dreading Monday.

So, What Can Be Done to Make Teaching and Learning More Personalized?

The most obvious solution currently available to us is computers. Using technology to personalize teaching and learning is an approach that has proved somewhat contentious, and its benefits have not been proven, but in terms of practical potential computers are pretty hard to beat. It's certainly enticing to think that there could be technology out there capable of drawing out children's skills and understanding at a precisely calibrated pace and with a precisely calibrated method of address.

Some people don't like the idea of pupils using computers too regularly. They see them as a necessary modern evil, acceptable for background research – "google" is a verb even for very young children these days – but not much more than that. The fear seems to be that classrooms kitted out too enthusiastically with computers will become dull, lifeless places with rows of automata silently staring at screens. As one well-respected UK education commentator, Phil Beadle, put it: "An inspiring education is a sensory joy, and the idiotic preeminence of the computer a denial of this." He fears that: " . . . if a computer can be used to personalize education, then there will eventually be no need for learning support in human form." (Beadle, 2008). We agree that an inspiring education is a sensory joy, but we disagree that using computers necessarily precludes this and that computers diminish the need for human learning support. Computerized personalization should support, not replace, school personnel (although some misguided political number-crunchers might think otherwise).

A more serious challenge is that computer-based teaching, even when highly individualized, has not yet been proven to increase achievement scores. In fact, a 2010 US Federal Review found that the computer-based instruction programs they assessed showed "no discernible effect" on students' SAT scores. It is important to education that new interventions are supported by evidence, and computer-based personalized learning methods have not yet satisfied the high standards of science. Nonetheless, there is cause for optimism that they might. For instance, there are scores of case studies in which teachers, schools, and even whole school districts report improvements among their pupils in terms of understanding, enjoyment, and ability, making it possible that the studies are not yet getting at what the teachers see on the ground.

It is disappointing that the software developed so far is not supported by scientific evidence, but we think that this should provide a spur to make such programs, and their implementation, more effective rather than ditch the approach as a whole. Until such approaches gain a strong scientific evidence base we would advise cautious enthusiasm and funding to improve the software, rather than a gung-ho spending spree. Personalization technology is a work in progress. It is an approach that has more potential for truly personalized education than any other currently available to us, and therefore it should be given the time and resources needed to improve.

Computers and software, when used well, should free up teachers and teaching assistants to support individual pupils more effectively. This approach is likely to be most successful in objectively assessed subjects such as mathematics. We do not for one moment suggest that all lessons should be computer-based. The most highly developed math instruction program we are aware of was created by Carnegie Learning, in conjunction with scientists at Pittsburgh's Carnegie Mellon University. The US Federal Review mentioned above did not find the Carnegie program to have statistically significant effects on achievement. However, many of the schools to have used it describe benefits. For example, Louisiana math teacher Krista Majors describes struggling students exposed to the program on Carnegie Learning's website:

> Students who were enrolled in the pilot class "caught up" with their peers enrolled in regular classes during the first year. They maintained that gain into the second year even though they were no longer enrolled in Carnegie classes. Most students in the control group, who were mixed in with the regular population, either stayed the same or fell further behind.

There is obviously work still to be done here to establish whether empirical support for this approach is forthcoming. However, it seems to us that the existing program has merits and may in time become a model for a teaching and learning strategy that will improve as a result of the research process. Its ability to respond to individual development is intriguing and it is not unreasonable to predict that such software will also eventually be able to interact with the Learning Chip technology that we discussed in Chapters 1 and 2. There's work to be done but we believe it to be work worth doing.

Carnegie Learning was founded by a team of cognitive scientists from Carnegie Mellon University in conjunction with a team of veteran math teachers. One of the founders was Professor John Anderson, best known for his development of a model of how the mind works, known as ACT-R. The aim of any cognitive architecture such as this is to define the fundamental cognitive and perceptual processes that make the mind work. ACT-R has done this successfully, and has been validated by hundreds of studies. This model of the mind underpins Carnegie Learning's

Math program by using *Cognitive Tutors* with an internal ACT-R model that can mimic the behavior of any pupil using the software. *Cognitive Tutors* can therefore personalize materials and "predict" the difficulties a particular pupil might have.

By recognizing individual differences, the fact that pupils develop, learn, and master math at different paces, this artificial intelligence-based approach can personalize the math learning environment of every pupil in a class. It can identify when a pupil is struggling or has not fully understood something and then customize prompts to focus on the area of weakness, providing new problems until the idea has been understood or the skill has been learned. There's no putting your hand up and waiting around when you're stuck, or giving up because "I just can't do it"; the software is capable of gently guiding pupils out of ruts, and supporting and encouraging them as they do so. It works like Personal Training – a source of expertise and encouragement by your side as you work to achieve your goals and your potential.

The Carnegie math program is rooted in findings from cognitive science, as described above, but it also draws on the body of research into mindset and motivation led by Professor Carol Dweck of Stanford University. In Chapter 7, we discussed the implications of this "mindset" research on the way that we praise and encourage our children in order to build their motivation and self-confidence. The Carnegie software does something similar by harnessing Dweck's findings to tailor the feedback that *Cognitive Tutors* provide to pupils.

A Good "Mindset" for Learning

In her books, talks, and papers Professor Dweck describes two types of "mindset": a fixed mindset and a growth mindset. Over the course of scores of experiments she and her colleagues and collaborators have shown how a growth mindset yields better results for everybody and, importantly, how the growth mindset can be taught. In light of this research the feedback given to pupils by Carnegie Learning's program is specifically designed to foster a growth mindset as a spur to mathematical development.

People with a fixed mindset believe that intelligence and talent are innate and cannot be changed. This leads to beliefs along the lines of "naturally clever or talented people shouldn't have to try" and "If I fail, people will think less of me." Dweck and her team have shown time and again that adults and children with this mindset shy away from challenges because they don't believe they can learn to do what doesn't come naturally to them; they don't want to make an effort because having to do so undermines their self-worth; and moving from their comfort zone puts them at risk of what they see as failure, and this is intolerable to them. This perhaps explains why some pupils who perform very well in English write themselves off in math, and vice versa – their self-concept can't cope with the fact that success doesn't come effortlessly. The generalist genes hypothesis suggests that a pupil who is extremely able in English is likely to be at least reasonably good at math, and yet such pupils, if they have fixed mindsets, are likely to write themselves off as hopeless just because they fall short of exceptional. As a result these people, even when highly able and talented, often plateau and live a life in which they operate well below their full potential.

Many pupils have fixed mindsets, some from very young ages. Dweck argues that they mostly acquire these beliefs from the people around them – their parents and, later, their teachers. However, we suspect that such beliefs are also a marker for genetically influenced temperament: we hope to explore this in our own future research. We think it is likely that, for genetic as well as environmental reasons, it will be harder for some people to develop a growth mindset than others. However, Dweck has lots of good ideas about how to help a child with a fixed mindset to develop a growth mindset. Her suggestions form the basis of an educational software program she has developed, called *Brainology*. The *Brainology* software is another means of connecting with individual pupils to raise achievement and, again, shows the advantages of learning from a computer at least some of the time. A computer, for example, talks to you alone. You can pause or repeat lessons whenever you like and as often as you like. You're not having to keep pace with 29 other pupils.

A child with a growth mindset loves a challenge. Dweck first became interested in this whole area when she was researching different people's responses to failure. She was surprised to see that some children, when confronted with a puzzle that was very difficult for them, didn't see that as failure. She saw from their responses that rather than feeling as though they were failing when they couldn't do something straight away, they felt as though they were learning. She describes her own initial (fixed mindset) reaction to these kids: "*What's wrong with them? I wondered. I always thought you coped with failure or you didn't cope with failure. I never thought anyone loved failure. Were these alien children or were they on to something?*" Children (and adults) with a growth mindset know that hard work pays off. Dweck and her team asked people of all ages a simple question: "When do you feel smart?" The fixed mindsetters said it was when they didn't make any mistakes; when they finished something fast and it was perfect; or when they found something easy that other people couldn't do. The responses of those with a growth mindset were very different. They said they felt clever when they tried really hard and managed to do something they couldn't do before. Dweck's findings are, we think, hugely important to education and parenting. The programmers at Carnegie Learning were well advised to take this research on board in designing their personalized math software, as "mindset" appears to provide a unique perspective on pupils' learning triggers.

It turns out that lots of parents and lots of teachers, encouraged by the self-esteem movement that bulldozed its way through child development in the late twentieth century, are getting it wrong. Every time we tell a child "I can't believe you got another A – you're so clever!"; "You're a natural – you're going to go far!"; or "You were robbed – you were easily the best and you should have won," we encourage a fixed mindset. What starts out as a simple attempt to make the child feel good and bolster their self-confidence inadvertently harms their ability to achieve their full potential. If we praise them for ability they won't want to risk failure. And this is not just opinion – Dweck has a whole series of compelling studies which support her advice. Instead we should praise children for effort, or for trying different approaches to solving a problem, identifying strategies for overcoming hurdles. If a child completes a task fast and perfectly they learn nothing from it – the task is simply too easy for them. It happens all the time, but Dweck suggests that rather than giving the child a sticker or a certificate and telling them how great they are the teacher or parent should apologize to them for wasting their time and promise to find a more suitable task next time. Carnegie's software automatically guides such a child to the next level in mathematics and offers some of the early support they need in learning the new skills involved. Equally, it encourages and supports pupils who are struggling in ways that praise small steps forward and encourage perseverance.

Children do best when they are working just outside of their comfort zone, having to scrabble a little to reach the next level. Children with a fixed mindset will find this desperately uncomfortable and want to back away, so the teachers and parents around them should respond by praising effort, concentration, persistence, and all of the other qualities that keep them at it until they get the buzz of achieving something they didn't know how to do before. The Carnegie program promotes a growth mindset by giving feedback that focuses on effort and progress and via "Messages of the Day" that include facts about how the brain changes and grows as students learn. They show pupils that the brain is a muscle that can be strengthened via exercise, namely hard work and perseverance. Perhaps one of the ways the Carnegie software could be improved to meet the high standards of scientific testing would be to further personalize these messages, to trigger positive genotype–environment correlations by giving individual kids more precisely targeted praise and encouragement. The fixed mindsetters, for instance, are likely to need a different approach to those who already have a growth mindset. Some will be tougher nuts to crack than others, and software that can recognize this and respond appropriately may represent progress for both the child and the teaching method. Dweck's "mindset" research has widespread implications for education.

Carnegie Learning's ACT-R-based math instruction program is just one example of the personalization software already available to educators. We do not recommend that all schools rush out and buy it, or current alternatives to it, because it is not at all unreasonable to expect such a program to prove its worth in the form of objectively assessed improved achievement. It has not yet accomplished this. It is important, though, that some schools trial these approaches, so that they can be refined and assessed. The fact remains that software such as this can potentially help to guide a child through the math curriculum at their own pace, and can facilitate progress in a way that a teacher alone cannot, by literally providing 30 different lessons to 30 different pupils. In short, it is capable of much of what personalized instruction should be, and therefore capable of making personalized teaching practically possible. In an ideal world, educational decision makers at a national level would support such software developers. In order to assess their effectiveness for example, it would help if they were linked to national tests. It would also help if adequate funding was provided for professional development so that teachers are properly taught how to integrate such software into their lessons.

Computers offer personalization technology but they also offer choice and, importantly, access to education. Stanford University professor, Sebastian Thrun, recently bemoaned the fact that his Artificial Intelligence classes were only reaching the 200 or so students that were enrolled on his course. Not being the sort of person to sigh and shrug and do nothing he developed an online version of the course. Since its inception he has enrolled 160,000 students and now, through *Udacity*, a private company he has founded, he offers 11 courses to students from, according to Thrun, every country in the world except North Korea. He says his costs, roughly, are $1 per student per class and, at this point Udacity's courses, examinations, and certification are offered free of charge. Courses such as Thrun's are known as MOOCs (Massive Open Online Courses) and are increasing in number. 2012 was designated

"The Year of the MOOC." At a time when organizations like UNESCO are spearheading the spread of education throughout the world, initiatives such as this one have to be of interest as a means of providing a university-level education to interested students who could never otherwise afford one. It is interesting that of the students who sat Thrun's first examination the top 410 exam performers were not Stanford students but simply interested people who had signed up online. In the democratization of education it seems highly likely that computers will play a major part. The work ahead involves finessing products and processes, and establishing validity and proof of effectiveness.

Other Ways to Personalize Learning

Of course personalized learning cannot begin and end with computers, and if we were privileged with a bird's-eye view of what goes on in every classroom every minute of every day we would see many, many examples of personalization in practice. There are wonderful, sensitive, and highly skilled teachers out there, in great numbers, who draw out the best from individual children all the time. The difficulty lies in doing it for all children at the same time. We need to focus on identifying what works for individual children and testing whether it could work more widely and whether it can stand up to the rigors of scientific proof. When we find initiatives that meet these criteria they should be rolled out to everybody, so that all schools, teachers, and pupils can benefit from good practice. In our own experience – both personal and professional – we have come across approaches to personalization that really do appear to work, approaches on which we would be prepared to structure testable hypotheses.

Joined-up thinking is sorely needed here if we are to pool all of the personalization practices out there and scientifically test their effectiveness. The US-based "What Works Clearinghouse" attempts to achieve exactly this. Created in 2002, it gathers educational research together in one place and clearly shows the degree to which particular educational methods are supported by good scientific evidence. The University of York's Institute for Effective Education represents a related initiative in the United Kingdom, and there is a "What Works" agenda gaining momentum in government too. However, systems such as these can only be as good as the research that's out there, and there is a responsibility to fund well-designed studies of any education intervention that shows promise. It will be important that at least some of these studies are genetically sensitive. Seeking scientific evidence of effectiveness is a step that is too often missed out because it takes time and money, and a government with a four-year term wants to make as big and quick a splash as possible, for as little cash as possible. This is short-sighted, and is the reason that education should be a cross-party domain that cannot be disrupted by changes of government. If we put time into finding what works, implementing it, and then allowing it to bed down and flourish over as many years as it needs, we will benefit as individuals and as a society. Taking your best guess, spending taxpayers' money, irritating teachers, and then withdrawing the intervention because of teething problems really doesn't work.

In Summary . . .

And so, let's not abandon our frustrated teacher, dragging her feet as she walks out to the school car park racking her brain for something to put in her "personalization improvement plan." We would suggest one simple step: turn the page. In the next chapter there are 11 ideas that take into account everything that we have discussed in this book so far – all genetically sensitive and all as practical as possible. Together they explore ways – some old, some new – of introducing personalization to every classroom in the country. How about that for a personalization improvement plan?

References

Beadle, P. (2008). A step too far. *The Guardian*, 1 April 2008.
http://www.carnegielearning.com/ (accessed 17 June 2013).

Further Reading

For an interesting approach to personalized learning, using technology among other methods, read this article about the "School of One":

http://www.theatlantic.com/magazine/archive/2010/07/the-littlest-schoolhouse/308132/1/ (accessed 17 June 2013);

and watch this video:

http://schoolofone.org/concept_introvideos.html?playVideo (accessed 17 June 2013).

Chapter 13

Eleven Policy Ideas

In this chapter we present our wish list. We describe eleven ideas that represent our current interpretation of how we might put genetically sensitive findings about education and learning into practice. If tested and found to be effective – an essential step in the process – we think these ideas might make schools better places for the children who learn in them, the teachers who work in them, and the society that pays for them.

1. Minimize the Core Curriculum and Test Basic Skills

Genetic basis: *We are all different.*

Recommendation: *Mandatory subjects should be kept to a minimum (one size does not fit all). The National Curriculum should only cover the "Basic Skills" of reading, writing, numeracy, and*

G is for Genes: The Impact of Genetics on Education and Achievement, First Edition.
Kathryn Asbury and Robert Plomin.
© 2014 John Wiley & Sons, Inc. Published 2014 by John Wiley & Sons, Inc.

ICT (defined as those skills required to live successfully in society). For all except the profoundly disabled, passing a final Basic Skills examination – based on this National Curriculum - will be a condition of leaving school.

There are certain skills that children need to learn in order to become independent adults, namely reading, writing, numeracy, and ICT. We also know that prior achievement predicts future achievement and that these skills are what early achievement consists of, and represent the building blocks for almost all areas of learning. Without them, many paths are closed off to young people. We have already clearly stated our view that education fails if it leaves children without confident mastery of these basic skills for life. This is not, however, an argument against "knowledge"-based education, as our other ideas should make clear.

Genetic and environmental effects mean that some kids will have a hard time acquiring these skills while others will pick them up almost instinctively without much external input at all. However, we must remember that the abnormal is normal and that the children who find mastery of these skills difficult are, in almost all cases, not genetically distinct from other children. There is no genetic reason why they cannot succeed given personalized support. These pupils need to be taught in a way that makes sense to them, and their precise level of understanding at the beginning of the learning process has to be identified in order for education and skill formation to progress in a logical, hierarchical sequence. Supporting these children should be the top priority for all schools.

Our research, and that of educational researchers throughout the world, suggests that children learn in different ways and at different paces. (In time, Learning Chips may help us to understand the etiology of these differences.) Therefore, we recommend designing a series of basic skills levels to be worked through by all children, culminating in a final pass/fail certificate test, which individual pupils can take whenever they and their teachers feel they are ready. Schools should encourage a growth mindset by encouraging perseverance in subjects that pupils find difficult, particularly when those subjects are core basic skills. If pupils find everything they do easy then they are not learning, merely enjoying the status quo. Carol Dweck's mindset research shows us that pupils learn best when they learn how to tolerate operating just slightly above their comfort zone. For this reason, all pupils will continue to develop their literacy and numeracy skills even if they complete their compulsory basic skills examinations early.

We would seek advice on establishing the appropriate minimum threshold for passing this certificate. Some very able children will complete all of the basic skills levels and the final test early and move on to more difficult literacy and numeracy classes, while some will work on learning and consolidating the basics throughout their education. The only stipulation is that a pass in the final basic skills certificate must be achieved before any pupil leaves school, even if this involves keeping a minority of pupils in school for an extra year. We believe that insistence on mastery of these basic skills for life will make pupils more attractive to employers and will have a wide-ranging positive influence on their quality of life, particularly for those who are less academically inclined. Because of this we believe, simply, that the children who need the most help should get the most help, and that the help they receive should be carefully tailored to their individual needs.

2. Increase Choice

Genetic basis: *Genotype–environment correlation depends on choice.*
Recommendation: *Increase the range of subject options available to all pupils, and give teachers more freedom in their lessons.*

We recommend offering a very wide range of options in all schools, alongside the compulsory basic skills. We believe that, particularly as pupils get older, it makes good genetic sense for them to have the opportunity to weight their education in favor of their passions and talents. We also believe that there should be much greater opportunity for primary school pupils to make choices and direct their own education. For instance, a child with a developing talent or interest in music, game design, sport, history, astronomy, or art should be able to use some of the school day to develop their interest or talent further, and should be able to access resources and (ideally) a teacher who can help them to develop their particular interests and talents. This "choosing time" is highly likely to require mixed-age classes. We will discuss some of the practicalities of this in the next chapter where we make our own first attempt at putting our ideas and recommendations into practice.

By not placing restrictions on what teachers can teach and how they can teach it in all areas beyond the acquisition and mastery of basic skills for life, we make space for personalization at the level of the class, small groups, and individuals. Good teachers will be able to draw on their own interests and strengths, in combination with those of their pupils, to plan lessons that are valuable and interesting. They will be able to spend extra time on topics that seem to work especially well without worrying about falling behind on a centrally directed syllabus or preparing for tests. Because the curriculum will no longer be centralized, any testing will be organized at the level of the school and will serve the sole purpose of reassuring teachers that their pupils are learning and progressing. When pupils reach the age of formal examinations they will follow syllabuses set by independent examination boards and selected by schools and teachers, just as they currently do. The results of the basic skills certificate test will reassure governments that schools are equipping pupils with the academic skills they need to become successful members of society and, from age 16 onwards, they will also have formal examination results.

Of course this recommendation is dependent on the recruitment of "good" teachers – teachers who have strong ideas about what they would like to teach; excellent listening and observation skills; and thoughtful ideas about how to personalize the learning experience for individuals with different profiles within a mixed classroom. They may be teachers with "growth mindsets." Their mindset could either be assessed with an aptitude test for candidates for teacher training courses, or taught as a key component of teacher training and assessed later by individual employers. Such teachers should be granted the autonomy to draw out the potential of their pupils in the way they see fit, and schools should be expected to offer their pupils a wide array of choices – something to stimulate every child.

3. Forget About Labels

Genetic basis: *The abnormal is normal.*
Recommendation: *If children need extra help, just give it to them. There's no need for all the labels and bureaucracy.*

Common learning problems are not qualitative disorders, just quantitative dimensions. In most instances the lowest-performing pupils are not genetically distinct from the rest of the class; they should be regarded as having a difficulty rather than a disability. This applies to some of the most common learning problems, such as dyslexia and dyscalculia. At the moment, it is expected that a low-performing child should be referred for assessment, given a label, and only then given support. Where resources are tight it is not unusual for parents to be left in a position where they have to pay for private assessments and tuition. Valuable time is lost in this process and it is likely that the stress it causes is bad for all involved.

Instead we would recommend that the observation and tracking process is intensified for children who are falling behind in a basic skills for life area, and that these children receive individualized support in the school setting as soon as concerns are raised. Resources should be focused on providing these children with all of the support and extra education that they need to stay on track. The principles of hierarchical learning should be employed to ensure that new skills build on existing skills in steps that are manageable for the individual child. Where possible, the family should also be enlisted to support the child's learning, with tangible tasks, but if this does not happen the child should not be penalized in any way. For instance, it is not uncommon for primary school teachers to change reading books only after they have been read to parents at home. Where parents are under-involved this can mean that some children have less opportunity to read aloud and less exposure to new books. These children's reading needs to be heard more often in school to make up for the deficit at home, while at the same time efforts should be made to entice parents to engage with the process. Children should never be penalized for their parents' problems or inadequacies.

We also recommend that labeling children as "Gifted and Talented" is stopped. In a personalized classroom the label is unnecessary as each child should have their individual needs met. Appropriate opportunities should be offered to all children and, in the ideal scenario, every child will be found to have a gift, a talent, or a passion worth nurturing. The time spent in identifying, labeling, and counting "Gifted and Talented" children is wasted time that could be spent on drawing out the potential of every child in the class.

The bottom line is that bureaucracy and labeling should be reduced so that children who struggle at any point in their education – even if turns out to be a transient problem – receive the extra support they need as soon as they need it. Any ongoing difficulty can be recorded on the personalized school-leaving certificate we recommend each pupil receives (see Recommendation 4), so that their needs can be recognized and accommodated by future educators and employers. Children who excel should also be offered the support and opportunities they need as a matter of course.

4. Teach the Child, As Well As the Class

Genetic basis: *Genetic continuity and environmental change can be monitored.*

Recommendation: *Each pupil should have an Individual Education Plan which should be reviewed and revised each year. Every child should receive a personalized school-leaving certificate at the end of their compulsory education.*

We propose that before every child starts school they are visited at home by the teacher who will be in charge of their first class, and a trained key-worker. This key-worker will take overall responsibility for observing, tracking, and generally looking out for the child throughout their school journey. This visit will be the first opportunity for the family and the school to learn about each other and about the individual child. Ability can be observed in this setting, or separately at school, and a developmental checklist can be completed in order to get a clear view of the child's school readiness and their particular needs and developmental profile.

After the visit the child's key-worker will draw up an Individual Education Plan (IEP) for the child's first term that can be revised in consultation with the teacher and the child's family. In the first year of education the IEP will be revised again after Christmas, taking into account the child's adjustment to school, and from this point it will be revised annually, during the summer holiday, unless an interim review is deemed necessary. The child's key-worker will be the first point of contact for the child, the family, and the class teacher throughout school, and will be expected to have a good knowledge of the child's needs, motives, and background. Even as class teachers change, the key-worker will remain the same and this continuity of care will do much to make a personal approach to education possible. The child will have an advocate within the school who has a strong understanding of their needs and their educational and family history.

The system will really come into its own at the level of secondary education, where pupils often have so many teachers that nobody knows individual children especially well. The key-worker will, for example, draw reports from subject teachers together and put them in the context of the whole child, spotting any new patterns or causes for concern immediately. This key-worker should also be able to advise class teachers on the best way of working with the individual children in their caseload, and the means of getting the best from them. They will document this information and their related suggestions and ideas in the annual IEP.

Our recommendation is based on the belief, drawn from our research, that every child has special educational needs of some type or at some point, and that these need to be closely monitored and responded to in order to support children in developing fully and achieving at a level that is fulfilling for them. We recommend that every school has its own substantial team of educational psychologists, and that these professionals are trained to provide the key-worker role. In this capacity they will assess, understand, and communicate educational and ability profiles; communicate with children and families; and be trained in counseling techniques in order to be able to support pupils who need this service. They will also coordinate the extra resources needed by a particular child, and in time they will incorporate genetic information drawn from each child's DNA sequence into their "big picture" of each child's needs. We believe this is a better use of a highly trained and skilled workforce than the current approach in which they are employed by local government bodies and spend much of their day driving between different schools, filling in paperwork, and fighting bureaucracy. We believe the service they can offer children in this key-worker role, and their ability to enhance personalization in education, could be second-to-none and could make a very positive difference to children's achievement, wellbeing, and lifelong prospects.

5. Teach Children How To Succeed

Genetic basis: *IQ and self-confidence may mediate the relationship between the school environment and achievement through a process of genotype–environment correlation.*

Recommendation: *Introduce a weekly Thinking Skills session for all pupils. (Thinking Skills will not be a National Curriculum subject as the syllabus will not be dictated from the center and there will be no public examinations associated with it. Schools will simply commit to spending one hour per week on Thinking Skills.)*

Research so far suggests that the process of genotype–environment correlation may be influential in mediating the relationship between an environment, such as teacher quality, bullying, or class size and an outcome, such as achievement. Active correlations in which pupils' genetically influenced traits – for instance, their IQ, motivation, or self-confidence – affect the relationship between an environment and an outcome constitute a major research priority for behavioral genetics. When we have a fuller understanding of this phenomenon, and better tools for measuring it, our ability to recommend educational interventions that make sense for individual children will increase exponentially. In the meantime, we know that potentially mediating traits such as IQ and self-confidence have a stronger relationship with achievement than most of the environments we have looked at so far. We hypothesize a chain-reaction in which environments influence these mediating traits (as well as genes) and thereby affect the end result.

Everything we have learned so far has shown us that a high IQ and self-confidence have a positive impact on education, and that both are subject to genetic and environmental influences. We also know that with appropriate coaching they can be improved. Therefore, we recommend a weekly Thinking Skills session for every pupil in every school, focusing on these traits. We know that both of these traits predict good lifelong outcomes and that they are influenced by the environment as well as genes, making them perfect for educational intervention. In many private schools children already have regular training sessions in aspects of IQ testing, such as verbal and nonverbal skills. Many others are coached privately to prepare for school entrance exams which, in many instances, are essentially IQ tests. Thinking Skills sessions in every school will level the playing field, and research indicates that both pupils and society will benefit. We recommend that a wide range of resources including puzzles and philosophy exercises should be designed and made available for any teacher seeking inspiration and resources. Within schools, teachers can use IQ tests and psychological measures of confidence and motivation to assess whether pupils are making progress in these areas. The results should be kept on file by key-workers as part of each child's developing profile, and used for the child's benefit rather than as a marker of school or teacher quality.

6. Promote Equal Opportunities from an Early Age as a Foundation for Social Mobility in the Future

Genetic basis: *Preschool children are especially susceptible to the effects of shared environment.*

Recommendation: *Offer free, high-quality preschool education to disadvantaged children from age 2, free, high-quality preschool education to all children from age 3 to 4, and extra support to children in low-SES families from birth.*

This recommendation supports the findings of the UK based EPPE study as well as Heckman's economic findings, and is broadly supportive of current government policy in the United States, the United Kingdom, and elsewhere in the developed world. We support this approach because it is consistent with the behavioral genetic findings that shared environment has significant influence on preschool children and that toxic environments, the homes that a minority of particularly vulnerable children grow up in, are especially powerful. Free, high-quality preschool education for disadvantaged children, therefore, has the potential to go some way towards equalizing learning opportunities. As with schools these preschools need to focus on developing and supporting individual children. Delaying formal learning does not have a negative effect in countries where it is the norm. For this reason we do not think that the focus of preschool needs to be on reading, unless that is what a particular child seems to crave. However, a focus on developing a growth mindset, IQ, social, and thinking skills, and self confidence, would seem to be a good idea. Preschools should be used to enhance school-readiness for all children and by making

high-quality preschool free for disadvantaged families – the kinds
of preschools that middle-class families will also be clamoring
to send their children to – we will contribute towards our aim
of equalizing opportunities. Even though shared environmental
influence wanes as pupils get older there is evidence that some of
the benefits may persist.

In addition to these measures, children from low-SES families
should be offered extra support from birth. Behavioral genetics
teaches that all human beings are born different and that differences in our environments – our nurture – increase the differences
we are born with. This is usually a negative thing, born of inequality of opportunity, but we propose that it doesn't have to be. In
fact, we can use environmental differences, and their effects, to
reverse the tide and enhance equality of opportunity. By offering
more opportunities to children in disadvantaged families, and
making it easy for them to take up the opportunities, we can make
progress in leveling the playing field and increasing social mobility.

We have several ideas for how to do this, although we look
to those who work closely with disadvantaged families for more.
Our ideas are designed mainly to start a debate about the kind
of education system that fosters equal opportunities and offers
a genuinely personalized learning environment to all children,
whatever their social, genetic, or developmental starting point. So,
for example, we recommend the development of a Portage-like
service aimed at all children growing up in disadvantaged families.
These children would receive regular home visits in which play-
based activities to assist and consolidate their development would
be introduced to them and to their parents. The approach will, we
believe, enhance skill development and school-readiness; support
parents in helping their children by modeling good practice to
them, thereby fostering stimulating home learning environments;
and encourage the development of a growth mindset, a can-do
attitude, and self-confidence from a very early age. The Portage
home visitor should remain in contact with the family throughout
the preschool period, until they hand over to a key-worker when
the child starts school.

7. Equalize Extracurricular Opportunities at School

Genetic basis: *Genotype–environment correlations depend on access to choice.*

Recommendation: *Level the playing field for extracurricular activities by providing extra support to pupils from families with fewer resources.*

One of the ways in which the playing field is not currently level is in access to extracurricular activities. A child with the potential to be a jockey, for example, who grows up in a city with a family of modest means will probably never discover his potential because horse-riding lessons and access to horses is prohibitively expensive.

The same is true for the child who could have been a pianist, a rock climber, or a ballet dancer. Lack of funds gets in the way of equality of opportunity and so does parental will and ability to get children to and from extracurricular activities. It's too hard if both parents have to work and don't have the right sort of childcare; don't drive; have several children; or suffer from disabilities. However, this is one of the ways in which potential is wasted and, therefore, one of the ways in which education can be used to draw out individual strengths and passions. We propose that the children of poorer families are provided with vouchers that can be exchanged for extracurricular activities based in schools or elsewhere. By basing more high-quality private lessons on school sites we would probably ensure better access for families and this, therefore, would be our preference.

8. Create a Two Stage PE Program

Genetic basis: *Shared environmental experiences have a significant impact on fitness for children in primary school, but genes then become more influential.*

Recommendation: *Set a standardized PE program for all children in primary school and Year 7, then allow children in*

Year 8 and above to choose the form of exercise that they will undertake.

The research we reported in Chapter 5 strongly suggests that shared environmental experiences have a significant impact on fitness for boys and girls in primary schools. This finding, combined with a rising obesity problem and an increase in diseases related to a sedentary lifestyle lies behind our recommendation that physical education should continue to be a compulsory subject in primary schools. It also suggests that at some point in the teenage years genes take over the driver's seat for both boys and girls. We therefore recommend that in the UK, alongside the National Curriculum PE lesson each week in primary schools, all pupils are exposed to a second session in which they can choose the activity they wish to pursue from a wide array of choices. Once again, this will require mixed-age PE groups. In this way pupils can identify the activities they enjoy most and develop some skill in them before they go to secondary school.

After the first year of secondary education the PE curriculum should be entirely choice-driven, again with a very wide array of choices. There should be no more compulsory cross country running in the rain, and no more humiliating football or netball sessions for kids who simply hate these sports. Individual differences in preference and ability will be respected in the new system. Pupils can choose to participate in whatever form of exercise they like best. The only rule is that they have to choose and commit to something. The evidence that exercise, perhaps particularly team-based exercise, may also interact with genes to militate against developing a lifelong smoking habit with all of its negative health implications, suggests that this recommendation may have a positive impact on health and health economics, as well as benefiting the individuals involved.

9. Change the Destination

Genetic basis: *Realizing genetic potential across a nation requires variety of opportunity beyond secondary education.*

Recommendation: *Increase the number and range of options available for work- and college-based vocational training; make apprenticeships more affordable for and attractive to employers; and educate pupils so they have mastered basic skills, found their true interests, and are more attractive to employers.*

Not everyone wants to go to university and, unfashionable though it is to say so, not everybody should. There are millions of students who will gain more life satisfaction, and in time earn more money, by mastering a set of skills that do not involve a university degree. In the United Kingdom the school-leaving age was raised from 16 to 17 in 2013 and will rise to 18 by 2015. We believe this change could benefit young people and society, but only if it offers young people education that actually meets their needs, interests, abilities, and aspirations. By offering "more of the same" to pupils who are switched off by academic study we will turn schools into holding-pens that cause more unrest than they solve.

By the later school years, if our recommendations are adopted, most pupils will already have achieved a pass in basic skills; they will have a developmental profile going back to before they began primary school; and they will have a key-worker who knows them well. This information could then be used to provide career and training advice to the individuals involved and to determine the courses that schools will offer to their older pupils. The child who wants to become a cabinet maker, a mechanic, a police officer, a healthcare assistant, a teaching assistant, or a receptionist should be given as much opportunity to pursue an education that will be useful to them as they try to achieve their aspirations as the child who wants, and needs, to go to university in order to become a lawyer, a doctor, or an engineer. A wide range of valuable and accredited courses that will prove genuinely useful to young people as they seek employment should be offered in every school and supported by at least as much funding as academic subjects. These pupils will not require further funding at university and so the final years of the school are the time to invest heavily in them and their plans for the future. Furthermore, and we appreciate that this is not easy to achieve in the current climate, they should have equal status in the school environment, an assertion which is borne of an understanding that they are following courses they have chosen rather than taking "second best" options because they weren't bright enough to do anything else. Education policy for many years has whittled away respect for choices that do not take pupils to university. Respect for individual differences in talents and preference needs to be restored, and parents and teachers bear a large part of the responsibility for restoring it.

In addition to offering all young people choices in line with their developing abilities and preferences, and basing their education on a cornerstone of basic skills, governments need to work with employers to provide apprenticeships, internships, work experience, and on-the-job training for all pupils who prefer to enter the world of work rather than the world of higher education.

10. Train New Teachers in Genetics and Give Them the Tools to Put it Into Practice

Genetic basis: *Personalizing education is the best way to realize the potential of individual children who are "naturally" different.*

Recommendation: *Add a course in the genetics of learning and education for all in teacher training, and issue a call for tender for groups and individuals who wish to design and pilot practical approaches to the personalization of education. Successful techniques, training, and resources should subsequently be made available to all schools.*

We recommend that all teacher-training courses include at least one module on the genetics of ability and achievement and the implications of individual differences for teaching practice. In this way we begin to tackle the assumption that children are blank slates who only need good enough teachers to get them all to jump through the same hoops. We also get to engage teachers in thinking about personalization from their earliest days in the profession. We think this is important because it will change the questions that teachers ask when faced with a struggling child, or a child with difficult-to-manage behavior. It will enhance their ability to reflect on and improve their own practice. In a system in which teachers are not judged on every child meeting a certain threshold in a certain year, or progressing through a certain number of National Curriculum sublevels, it is important that they have means of tracking and supporting progress and potential. It is important that, hopefully in conjunction with the child's key-worker, they are free to think about Individual Education Plans for every child and have strategies at their fingertips for implementing them successfully in large, mixed classes.

We have some ideas about how to make genuine personalization work in classrooms. These include our proposal to use educational psychologists as school-based key-workers. We also believe that there is a huge role for computers to play in personalizing education. Computer software that is sensitive to individual ability and progress will, we predict, be the single biggest support to teachers trying to personalize the learning experience in mixed classrooms. Ever-greater use of interactive technologies will increase the possibilities for all children to be making progress, even at times when the teacher does not have the resources to move them on. Our focus on ICT as a Basic Skills subject will support children in being able to benefit from educational software.

We ourselves do not presume to design the software or the myriad personalization interventions that are possible. We believe that this would be better done by teachers and educational software designers, and that government funding should be provided to encourage this to happen and the results of well-designed and reliable studies of pilot interventions shared so that best practice in personalization can be implemented in all schools. In the meantime, we will focus on continuing to enrich the evidence base for individual differences in learning that we hope will inform these initiatives.

11. Big Is Beautiful

Genetic basis: *Genotype–environment interplay and nonshared environmental influence depend on choice.*

Recommendation: *Size makes choice viable. Make our schools bigger and the links between the different levels of schooling stronger.*

Everything we have learnt about individual differences, about genotype–environment interplay and about nonshared environmental influence points to choice as an integral element in offering equal environmental opportunities to all natures. In practice, economies of scale dictate that this necessitates large schools. Size will make choice economical and viable and choice is what matters. Schools, therefore, need to be big; to be capable of offering an unprecedentedly broad range of educational choices; and to be so desirable that everybody of every background wants to come. It is undemocratic to ban the competition – the schools that cream off the easiest pupils and claim their success as their own – so we just have to beat it. There are very few schools that could compete with one in which your child was offered a completely personalized learning experience from ABCs through to school-leaving or graduation, and in which they can pursue *any* learning goal you care to mention. Size will matter because we will need enough demand to justify the diverse supply of educational experiences we wish to offer. Genetically sensitive schools will be very large schools with continuity between primary, secondary, and tertiary education. There will be a place for all of the children in a single community in one of our genetically sensitive schools and, if it is properly designed and run, they will all want to come.

In the next chapter we imagine a school in a world where our wish list becomes law. We appoint ourselves Education Secretaries for a day.

Chapter 14

Education Secretary for a Day

As "Education Secretaries for a Day" we would graciously accept all eleven of our own policy ideas. Nonetheless, we would subject them to rigorous scientific testing and, if the results were positive, set up a genetically sensitive school. If our school worked well we would then roll out our plans across the nation. Either this is going to require a little suspension of disbelief or it's going to be a very long day. What we propose is a line-drawing of a genetically sensitive school. Much coloring-in remains to be done by researchers, teachers, and society at large. But it's a start, something to work with – we make no greater claims.

The site we choose for our genetically sensitive school will be enormous, more like a small university campus than a traditional school. It will have to be this size to hold all of the facilities it needs to accommodate and all of the options it needs to provide. It will serve the community around it, and we will make it so appealing and so successful, and we will foster such a pleasant environment and such a wonderful reputation, that every child of

G is for Genes: The Impact of Genetics on Education and Achievement, First Edition.
Kathryn Asbury and Robert Plomin.
© 2014 John Wiley & Sons, Inc. Published 2014 by John Wiley & Sons, Inc.

every faith, every race, and every social background will want to be educated there. Our school site will need to be big so that we need turn away no child from our local community. There will be no complicated admissions procedure and no luck of the geographical draw. Our school will be built to accommodate every child in our local community, and in an ideal world every community will have an equivalent school. We are not unrealistic but this chapter is a place for utopian thinking rather than practicalities and caution. And since we're acting as politicians here we have a duty to actively sell the idea to you.

On the site we will build a primary school, a secondary school, and a linked center for children with special educational needs (who may be educated entirely there, entirely in mainstream school, or in some combination of the two). The degree of integration in classes for children with learning or behavioral difficulties will depend on the individual child's needs and wishes, but social integration will be improved simply by sharing a site and by sharing facilities. In this way we make children with disabilities part of the everyday world rather than hiding them away in physically segregated schools. We will also build a large and well-equipped leisure center with a pool and facilities for a broad array of sporting opportunities. There will be space for several sports fields and pitches and other outdoor facilities such as a horticulture center for aspiring botanists, beekeepers, landscapers, florists, and biologists. There will be a large and well-stocked on-site reference and lending library as well as music rooms, media rooms, language laboratories, and a theater. Finally, there will be a Child Development Center staffed by a General Practitioner or Primary Care Physician, a pediatrician, nurses, speech and language therapists, counselors, careers advisors, and our team of key-workers/educational psychologists. Other professionals such as physiotherapists and occupational therapists will be employed there too, as and when they are needed by our pupils.

All children will join our primary school with an Individual Education Plan (IEP), drawn up by the key-worker they will have met at home, together with their first teacher, in the months before they began school. In time, information will also be drawn from gene chip technology. The approach we take to learning at this stage will be based on the developmental profile underpinning the IEP. Reception classes will be play-based and will be set up to allow for intensive observation, monitoring, and tracking rather than formal instruction. Our Reception and Year One classes for 5- and 6-year-olds will be small – perhaps 15 to 20 children per class – to make a highly personalized education as easy to achieve as possible in the years when the basic skills are first introduced and in which children become accustomed to learning and socializing in the school environment. Teachers will focus on developing confidence and self-regulation skills as well as introducing children to formal learning when they are ready, and supporting their development in the social, creative, cognitive, and physical arenas.

Educational research has shown that small classes are most beneficial in these early years, underpinning our decision to make this investment young but not later. After the first two years class sizes will increase to a more typical 30 children. Research suggests that this is not harmful to pupils, and there is the added benefit that increased numbers can increase the likelihood of teachers being able to group children of like mind and like ability together for small-group teaching and peer-supported learning. By this time, age 7, the children who need extra support to master core educational skills will have been identified and, where appropriate, will have already been referred to the correct services in our on-site Child Development Center, as well as having their needs met in class. All children will have been exposed to some degree of formal instruction in the basic skills, although while some will be competent readers by this stage others will have begun their reading journey relatively recently. A teacher's referral to the Child Development Center for extra support, or their decision to provide one-to-one or small group tuition, will not have to be justified and will only be documented on the relevant children's IEPs.

As children progress through our primary school they will carry out focused activities in the 3Rs and ICT every day that reflect their individual goals. These goals will be defined by a National

Curriculum and progression towards passing the basic skills certificate. It is likely that these activities will take up most of the morning every day of the week, with space for self-directed play, learning, and observation in between focused activities. Once a week our children will take part in a National Curriculum PE lesson focused on fitness and health and once a week they will participate in a physical activity session of their own choosing, along with other primary school children from all years who have chosen the same option. The options could involve football, rugby, hockey, basketball, swimming, fencing, horse-riding, dance, archery, yoga, martial arts, skate-boarding, gymnastics, running, athletics, or anything else the student body suggests they would like to pursue. Lessons will be carried out in the school, the sports center, and the playing fields. They will be of sufficient structure and quality that, say, a child who commits to taekwondo will be able to work through the belts if they wish to and other children will be able to engage with their sport in terms of competitions or progressing through levels or grades. Choices and participation will be taken seriously and not viewed as "time out." This physical activity session will be one of two "choosing" sessions in the primary school week. Pupils can pursue the same activity throughout school if they wish to, or can choose different activities each term. Ideally they will identify and commit to a form of exercise they enjoy and are capable of progressing in by the end of their primary school education at age 11.

In addition to the weekly sports choice there will be a "choosing" afternoon once each week when children can select one option from a very wide range which they can pursue in a mixed age class with a teacher with the necessary expertise. Similar educational aims apply to this as to the sports session in that this will not be down-time. Rather, children will be observed and monitored just as rigorously in this session as in any other, and will be supported in developing their interest or skills further. The real purpose is to give our children plenty of opportunity to find their talents and interests, by trying out different activities and areas of learning, and to support them in developing their interest and their expertise.

Again, they will pursue their "choice" for at least one term before having the option to make another "choice."

In the remaining time, which will amount to approximately three afternoons, the teacher will be free to pursue the class's interests and needs in a series of more short-term "topics" and to use these sessions to focus on both whole class and individual learning goals. This time will also be spent on subjects such as nature, religion, thinking skills, art, music, drama, and humanities.

Topic sessions will represent an opportunity to pursue a particular subject in depth and to develop pupils' skills in art, music, drama, history, geography, science, and any other relevant subject. Our teachers will have total control over the topics they introduce to their classes, and the school will be sufficiently well-funded to support their choices with appropriate resources. Because all of the children will learn ICT skills from the very beginning of their education, the Internet will be a cost-effective way of providing children with access to relevant support materials without incurring too great an expense. This degree of flexibility was not possible when a single topic required the purchase of thirty books for a class, thereby committing generations of teachers to teaching the same material year after year, regardless of their own interests or those of their pupils. Teachers and pupils will have an unparalleled degree of degree of freedom to shape and direct their learning.

The basic structures of the primary school day will remain essentially unchanged; registration, mid-morning play, lunch and lunchtime play, and mid-afternoon play will punctuate the educational day. There will be assemblies and story time. The school day will be approximately 6 $1/2$ hours long.

After school, children will be free to sign up for a broad array of extracurricular activities, the cost of which will be means-tested, with the most disadvantaged children entitled to participate in any activity they choose free of charge. The school will hire specialist teachers for these extracurricular opportunities so that the quality is as good as would be provided privately. This is often not the case in schools for activities such as music lessons, and it will be important to provide teachers who have the time and capacity to really nurture talent or interest when they find it. These extracurricular activities will be open to children from the primary and secondary schools, including the center for children with special needs, and age restrictions will only be applied where absolutely necessary.

The primary school we have proposed differs from mainstream primary schools in some important ways. Learning will be personalized to an unprecedented extent by the involvement of the key-workers who will know and act as advocates for individual children. These key-workers will play a hugely important role in ensuring that every child's needs are understood in detail and are met at all times. They will speak up for the child when they need extra resources or support, and ensure that provisions are put in place to meet their individual needs. There is no doubt that our key-workers will provide a five-star service.

In part this is a nice way of saying it will cost a lot but it is important to bear in mind that improving education is likely to yield economic benefits to society as a whole, as well as supporting optimal child development. Our key-worker service is designed to provide lasting and life-enhancing benefits to every child, through making sure that their education is tailored, as perfectly as possible in the real world, to their individual needs. Any teacher who struggles with a child will have a point of contact with whom to discuss the child and devise strategies to improve their learning and their wellbeing. In the best-case scenario that point of contact will be an individual who has known the child since the age of 4 and has developed a strong relationship with them and their family over the intervening years. We will need to treat our key-workers well, and to set in place a career and pay structure that allows for personal progression. Our key-workers may not have access to a DNA screen for each child, although in time this will change, but they will have a clear understanding of the child's uniqueness – the behavioral manifestations of both their nature and their nurture.

When children reach the age of 11 they will make the transition to secondary school. Because our secondary school is on the same site as our primary school they will have already had many opportunities to visit the building and to interact with the teachers and pupils there. They will also be used to mixing with secondary school pupils in extracurricular activities and, in some instances, in the activities undertaken on their two "choosing" afternoons. Furthermore, their key-worker will stay with them through this transition and throughout their secondary school career. All of these factors will, we predict, enable a smooth transition for the vast majority of children.

In many ways, practices at the secondary school level will be similar to those at the primary school level. There may be some very able children who have already passed their final basic skills examinations but most others will still be working through the levels at their own pace as the final certificate will demand a good level of competence. After the first year of secondary school, National Curriculum PE will be replaced with a second one-hour sports option in which pupils can select an activity from the wide range on offer. As at the primary school level the whole school will undertake their PE sessions together so that as many options as possible can be offered to mixed-age groups. The same will apply to the second PE session of the week.

There will be some major differences though. For instance, we will take the opportunity when we open our school to trial a later start time, say 10 a.m., for our secondary school pupils. In an ideal world we will have already trialed this in an existing school – with a 9 a.m. start time for half of the pupils and a 10 a.m. start for the other half, so that we are certain about the decision we make. Scientific evidence suggests that teenagers' body clocks run several hours behind adults' because of differences in their melatonin levels that make them naturally unsuited to early starts. A 10 a.m. start has been tried in some schools and appears to be successful, or at least not harmful, but we would want to see the results of an experimental case control study of the change so that we ensure we offer the best and most appropriate education we can. If we do not trial the intervention prior to opening we will randomly assign our initial pupils to a 9 a.m. or a 10 a.m. start group, and will test their relative achievement, motivation, and wellbeing before making a final decision on school policy. We will also use the data to ask questions such as whether a late start, if it has a positive effect, is appropriate from age 11 or from a later age – say 13 or 14 – and whether a reversion to the earlier start-time should occur after 16. We will also consider the timing of formal examinations in light of the evidence. In our schools any new interventions will always be evidence-based and will always be subjected to an experimental trial before being adopted and implemented. A school designed on a scientific base, such as this one, must remain true to scientific evidence and the scientific method.

One major difference between our primary and secondary schools will be that pupils will be offered more individual choice in secondary school, and this will not be constrained to a single after-noon session. During their first year pupils will have compulsory classes – basic literacy, numeracy, and ICT skills, PE sessions, and science. During the first two years of secondary school they will be immersed in physics, chemistry, biology, and a course in under-standing and interpreting scientific findings, but will subsequently only be required to pursue one of these subjects to final examina-tion level. Many pupils will wish to pursue more, or even all, of the sciences and that will be their choice. Aside from these subjects 11- and 12-year-old pupils will be exposed to a broad array of taster courses, each lasting for a half-term or half-semester. At the end of their first year they will choose a selection of these courses to pursue the following year. The options will be defined by teacher and pupil interests. Pupils will have the same opportunity to stick with their choices or to change them in the following year, at the end of which they will choose the subjects that they will pursue for formal educational qualifications until the age of 16. The choices on offer will be academic: natural and social sciences, advanced mathematics, literacy, computing (beyond basic certificate level), humanities, modern and ancient languages, and arts subjects. They will also cover a wide range of vocational subjects that will prepare students, who we know will be literate, numerate, and able to use a computer, in the skills and knowledge they think they will need to secure the future to which they aspire. The range of options on offer will be unrivalled by those at any other school, something that will be made possible by our size as well as our prioritization of individual differences. All of our pupils will be free to choose a mixture of vocational and academic subjects if they, in consultation with their key-worker, their teachers, and their family believe that this is appropriate for them and will serve to activate positive genotype-environment correlations that will allow them to make optimal use of the opportunities on offer to achieve their ambitions and fulfill their natural potential.

It all comes down to choice (you see we're talking like politicians already). By offering an unprecedentedly large range of choices in both our curriculum and our extracurricular opportunities we will support pupils in pursuing a path through education that is tailor-made for them and will give them the skills, knowledge, and qualifications to go out into the world and succeed. Each pupil's key-worker will track their progress throughout school and access the support of professionals of any kind if and when they need them. In particular, all pupils will be offered high quality careers advice based on their individual profiles.

After formal examinations at age 16, pupils will move on to centers that will take them closer to achieving their ambitions. For some these will be colleges offering academic courses and aimed at preparation for university education, for others they will be well-funded vocational colleges with strong connections to employers, and with funding to train apprentices in the full range of trades and career paths. The colleges, rather than the individuals, will take responsibility for matching trainees with employers and will provide ongoing advocacy on behalf of the young people they teach in order to ensure that their training is well-funded and sufficiently diverse, so that nobody falls through the net.

Our genetically sensitive approach, although undoubtedly expensive, will support and nurture individual differences and will, we predict, prove both socially and economically beneficial to individuals and society in the long term. We believe this is an investment in education that is worth making and that will really make a difference. Average performance will go up and individual children will be better prepared to find useful and constructive ways of living in the world when they leave school. We aim to treat all children with equal respect and provide them with equal opportunities, but we do not believe that all our pupils are the same. Children come in all shapes and sizes, with all sorts of talents and personalities. It's time to use the lessons of behavioral genetics to create a school system that celebrates and encourages this wonderful diversity.

Index

G is for Genes: The Impact of Genetics on Education and Achievement, First Edition.
Kathryn Asbury and Robert Plomin.
© 2014 John Wiley & Sons, Inc. Published 2014 by John Wiley & Sons, Inc.

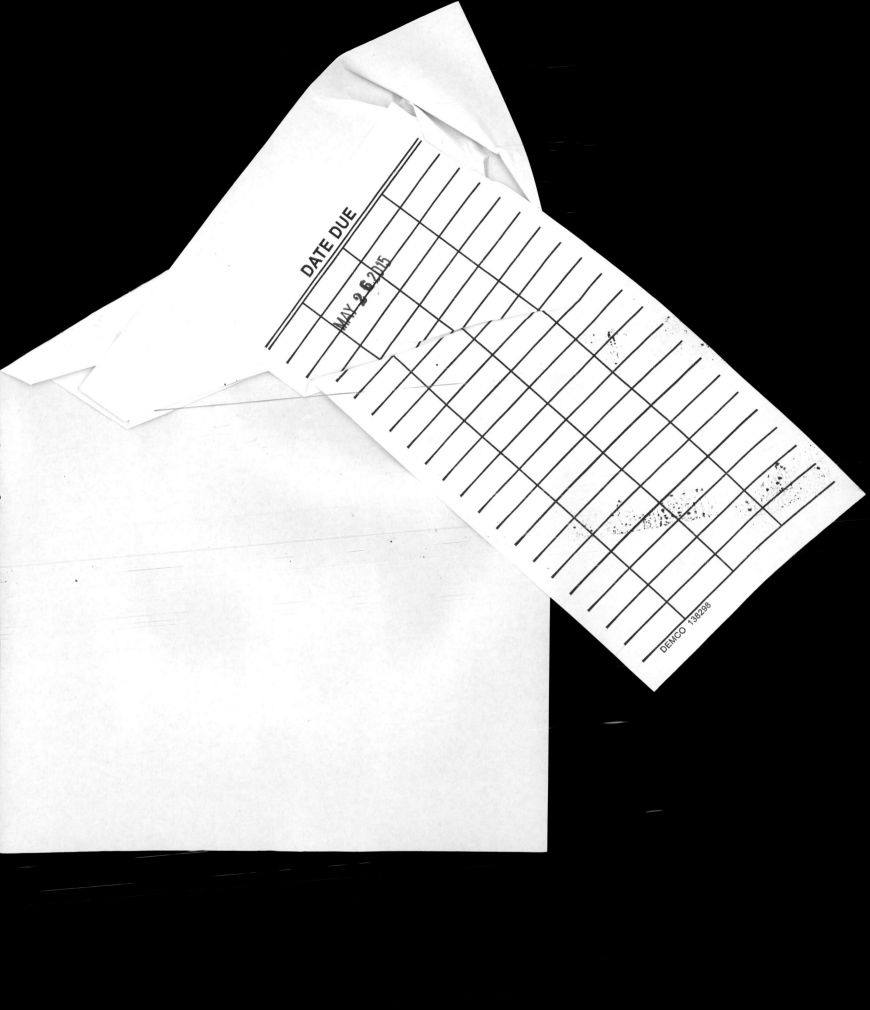